Astronomy Facts for Bright Young Minds

Elijah Stone

Table of Contents

Introduction

Have you ever wondered if we truly are the only living beings in the universe? Have you ever looked up at the stars and wondered what distant suns and planets they were? If you have, then you, like me, might just be a budding astronomer. "Oh, I know what an astronomer is," I can hear someone saying from the back. "They look at your star signs and tell your future, right?" Um, not quite. Astronomers do look at stars, but that has nothing to do with signs. Instead, they explore and try to understand the many, many suns, stars, planets, asteroids, and more that populate our galaxy and universe. They try to understand things like how our Earth and solar system formed, as well as how the universe came into being. Hint: It involved a rather big bang.

How do astronomers figure such things out? I mean, it's not like they have the Tardis or any other kind of time machine in their hands. So, it's not like they can jump back in time to watch all these things happen. Do you want to know the short answer to that question? It's technology. Scientists from around the world have developed incredible and wondrous machines and bits of technology to study space objects that are thousands, even millions, of light years away! From the Hubble Space Telescope to the Kepler Telescope, the tools they have at their fingertips are staggering.

Using these tools is a joy for scientists and astronauts, especially since it often leads to amazing new discoveries. Some of these technologies, for instance, have picked up the echoes of the Big Bang, which created the universe. Others, like Kepler, discovered planets that might be habitable and that, therefore, might have life! Still, others were used to figuring out how our sun was born and where black holes come from. As you'll discover in the pages of this book, these are just a few examples of the discoveries astronauts have made about space.

In the coming chapters, you're going to go on a very exciting adventure, one that begins with the Big Bang and stretches all the way to our current time, where we explore space in search of other habitable and maybe even cooler planets. As we make discoveries upon discoveries, you'll be introduced to all sorts of fun experiments that will help you understand some of what we've learned even better and have fun while doing so. You'll also come across a few art projects as well as a model-making venture! By the end of this book, you will not only understand your galaxy thoroughly but also be prepared to design your own! With that in mind, what do you say? Are you ready to go on an adventure across the cosmos?

Chapter 1:

The Amazing Story of Our

Universe's Big Bang

Did you know that the entire universe we live in began with a massive expansion called the Big Bang? Imagine that you blew a bubble. Only this isn't a regular bubble. It's about thousands of times smaller than the head of a needle. It's also much, much hotter than a regular bubble would be and really dense. By that, I obviously mean that the inside of the bubble is really full, almost bursting, and not that the bubble is dumb. Now, imagine what would happen to atoms, the particles that form all objects, including bubbles, if they encountered heat. They'd start moving about and knocking against one another, right? The more the heat increased, the faster those atoms would move until, finally, they'd crash against one another and burst forward to go in all sorts of directions. This is exactly what happens to our bubble. So, our heated bubble finally popped, and everything it had been containing—all those particles of life and the universe—would come spilling forward.

This is exactly what happened 14 billion years ago. Except our bubble did not go off with a soft pop. Instead, it went off with a massive bang, one so loud that scientists can still hear its echoes when they listen for it with the right equipment. When the explosion happened, everything contained within that dense little bubble burst forth. They spread out, grew, and expanded, and as they did, they wove together solar systems, galaxies, and the universe itself.

The Fascinating Mystery of the Big Bang

So, why exactly did this happen? After all, our bubble wasn't actually one. It was more of a dot—a single, very dense point. Nobody truly understands the composition of this point, and we probably won't discover it until we develop time-travel devices. What I do know is that at some point, that very dense and hot point exploded—about 10 billion degrees Fahrenheit, to be exact. When it did, the protons, neutrons, electrons, and raw materials that it contained spilled out. They stretched and expanded, moving at the speed of light, and settled into the void of space. In the process of cooking, they become a sort of galactic soup, so to speak. As time went on, electrons started knocking against other particles, creating atoms as they went. These atoms would become the building blocks of, well, everything.

Did you know that before atoms started forming, there was no light in the universe? Once atoms did come onto the scene, however, they became capable of capturing light. This wasn't an easy process, though. After all, just as it takes time for soup to cook, it takes time for atoms to actually form. So, while the Big Bang itself might have happened in about a few seconds' time, it took 380,000 years for light to come into existence, which is something to think about the next time you complain your parents are taking too long making your dinner.

The light that eventually took shape after the Big Bang is sometimes called the afterglow. If you want a more scientific name for it, as most scientists do, it's also called the cosmic microwave background (CBM), an odd choice of words, seeing as microwaves hadn't been invented yet and the first human wasn't even born by that point. Now, some of you might be wondering, "How do you really know all this?" It's not like we can travel back in time, as we said, and see all this unfolding in real-time. So, how can we know that the afterglow is a real thing?

The short answer to that question is, "Because Ralph Alpher said so." So, who's Ralph Alpher? Ralph Alpher was a cosmologist, i.e., a scientist who studied the cosmos. Alpher was very interested in the Big Bang Theory, because what would cosmologists not be? In 1948, he first came up with the concept of the afterglow. Two other cosmologists, Arno Penzias and Robert Wilson, confirmed his theory nearly 20 years later. Penzias and Wilson were working in a lab in New Jersey in 1965. In this lab, Penzias and Wilson constructed a radio receiver capable of detecting temperatures above normal but unable to produce music. As they used their new device, they encountered just such temperatures. Initially, they believed that a colony of pigeons, having established a nest in the device's massive antenna, was the cause of these temperatures. So, they did what they probably thought was a reasonable thing to do: they killed all the pigeons and used the device again. The temperature they were picking up remained the same.

What exactly does all this mean? It's simple, really: The Big Bang was so powerful that scientists are still able to observe its aftermath using the handy devices they've invented. That doesn't mean that the afterglow is still going on. It just means that we can still observe it. I can almost hear some of you going, "Huh?" So, think of it like this: Imagine that you are in a city square. The square is packed with people. Everyone there is asked to yell "Yay!" at precisely 3.15 p.m. For some reason, everyone agrees and yells out at the same time. You do as well. When you do, your voice fades away pretty quickly since it doesn't have much of a distance to cover before it reaches your ears. A full minute later, however, you can still hear screaming out, "Yays." This isn't because people are still screaming. It's because the "days" of the people farthest to you, say 165 feet away, are only now able to cover that distance and reach your ears. The same thing happens a full 10 minutes in, when "yays" from even farther away, say 250 feet away, reach your ears, though they do sound a lot softer than your scream and the screams of those closest to you. This is precisely how the afterglow works. It's also why we are still able to observe it, even if we have to squint.

The Cosmic Timeline

Have you ever done that admittedly slightly gross thing where you bite one end of the gum you've been chewing, pinch the other end between your fingers, and pull just to see how far it stretches? If you have, then you saw that gum can stretch pretty far. In this sense, chewed-up gum is a little like the universe: both can stretch pretty far. Except, of course, that stretched-out gum will break after a certain point. The universe, however, won't. At least, hopefully not. That's why it's been able to keep expanding even after all this time (Chown, 2024).

You heard that right: The universe is still expanding. So, if you were a space explorer, a space pirate, or something of the sort and wanted to discover the farthest reaches of the universe, you'd have to spend your whole life exploring. Even then, you wouldn't be able to map out the whole universe. How crazy is that? What if you were immortal? Could you do it then? Not necessarily, because despite what you might be expecting, the expansion of the universe hasn't slowed down a bit over the years. It has only grown! Allow me to explain: Imagine that you're holding a ball and that you throw it as fast as you can. The ball travels a good distance, but after a while, it starts losing speed. As the seconds tick by, the ball slows down more and more until it comes to a stop. Now, assume that that ball is the universe and that you're some kind of god, able to pick up and throw the universe. In this case, your ball, that is to say, our universe, wouldn't slow down no matter how much time passed. Instead, it'll keep going forever and ever. Not only that, but it'll pick up speed as it goes!

This is exactly what has happened with the speed at which the universe has been growing since the Big Bang. The bang served as the catalyst for growth. The growth has been non-stop, with no end in sight, and it has only picked up speed with each passing moment. So, you wonder, how fast is the universe expanding? Well... That's hard to say because scientists are currently in a bit of a disagreement over it. They're also in disagreement about how big the universe is. This is because even the biggest, most powerful telescopes can only see certain parts of the universe. They do not have the ability to see beyond those parts and so they cannot really measure what they cannot see!

The parts of the universe that good old scientists are able to see are those with stars, suns, and the like that they are able to observe. Here's a fun fact for you: If human beings had the ability to travel at lightspeed—or at warp speed, for my Star Trek fans—then we would actually be able to visit every single star that we can see! Sadly, we don't currently have that ability. So, all we can do for now is observe them from afar and ask a million questions while we're at it, like how the first elements of the universe formed. How on Earth—pun intended—did they eventually form into planets like the Earth?

To be honest, it took a while for elements to start forming in the universe. This is because the universe was a tad too hot and a tad too cold immediately after the Big Bang. The universe likes its contradictions, after all. Those elements only started appearing here and thereafter things had cooled off in some places and warmed up in others. Would you like to guess just how long that took? A year? A few hundred years? More? Don't worry, I'll wait... Alright, now that you've made your guess, let's see if you were right: It took precisely 380,000 years for the universe to cool down and warm up just enough to be just right, as Goldilocks would say, for elements to start forming (Klesman, 2018). Does that figure seem familiar? Well, it should! That also marked the generation of the universe's cosmic microwave background!

Clearly, that turning point 380,000 years ago was a big year for the universe. It was at this point, after all, that two key elements finally made their first appearance on the screen: helium, meaning that element that makes your voice funny when you inhale it, and hydrogen, which is a building block for water and, therefore, very necessary for life! Pretty soon, two other new elements joined this duo. These were lithium and beryllium. These two elements started mixing and mingling with helium and hydrogen within clouds of swirling cosmic dust and gases. These clouds cooled down even more as the universe kept stretching, and the elements within them started gathering close together. Slowly but surely, they built on top of one another and, over time, grew into planets, suns, moons, and entire galaxies! As they did, chemical reactions kept happening between them, and these resulted in the creation of even more elements. Some of these reactions even resulted in massive stellar explosions, which scientists later came to call supernovae, after human beings came into existence, of course.

Wait, how exactly can two to four elements create a galaxy? I can almost hear you asking this question, wondering how it makes sense. So, let's consider it together for a moment. Let's slow things down a bit and ask ourselves: What is a galaxy? How would you define it? Go ahead and try to come up with your own definition of it first:

_____

_____

However, you defined a galaxy just now, and you probably noted that it has at least a couple of solar systems in it. Solar systems, like the one we're a part of, have suns at their very centers, and various planets revolve around those suns, the way BTS fans revolve around BTS band members. A sun is basically a massive ball of fire. That massive ball of fire has a core, and that core is made up of just two elements: your old friend's helium and hydrogen, the first two elements to form in the universe! These two elements get into a number of different chemical reactions, or chemical fistfights, if you will. These fistfights create a lot of energy. To be exact, they create about 85% of all the energy a sun puts out (Krofcheck, 2009). The remaining 15%, as it happens, is generated by lithium and beryllium, the third and fourth elements to step onto the cosmic scene! Naturally, these elements get into chemical reactions with one another, as well as helium and hydrogen. In the process, they create so many things like ultraviolet light, X-rays, radio waves, microwaves, and visible light! A lot of these lights warm up the planets that circle around the sun, allowing life to flourish on them, the way they did with Earth, or so we think, as we haven't—yet— discovered any green aliens on other planets.

It isn't just fully grown, healthy stars that create chemical reactions and change in the universe. Dying ones do, as well. Wait, can the sun die? Yes, they can and do, though their lifespan is much, much longer than that of mere mortals. How do stars die, then? Do they cool down and wither away, like dried roses? Of course not. They go out with a literal bang, like the rock stars that they are. As we mentioned earlier, these massive explosions are known as supernovae, and these supernovae generate various new elements like oxygen, essential for human respiration, iron, gold, and uranium. When a supernova takes place, it doesn't just create these elements. It sends them careening throughout the universe, and they keep going and going until they collide with something, like another element, and join hands with it in a chemical reaction, creating something entirely new in the process.

That explains how the sun and solar systems came to be, but what about planets like Earth? How exactly did they form? How about the moon, for that matter? Remember how we mentioned that the Big Bang created these swirling dust clouds that spread out across the universe? Well, over time, the particles making up those dust clouds joined together and turned into clumps of dirt. Those clumps grew bigger and bigger until they formed... If you finish that sentence with "planets," I'm sorry, but you are wrong because they first formed something called "planetesimals." Planetesimals are bite-sized planets, though by bite-sized, I mean that they're a couple of hundred miles across. So, you can't exactly eat them if you want to. As time went by and more dust kept swirling around those planetesimals, they grew into...protoplanets. These protoplanets were about the size of Mars, and given their size and closeness to one another within the same dust cloud, they started colliding with one another pretty soon. After enough collisions, they became stuck together, too. Thus, protoplanets are added on top of one another to form a massive planet, and the same ice cream scoops are added on top of one another to form one massive ice cream, allowing you to tell your parents you only had one scoop without lying.

After numerous collisions, the Earth came to be the exact size it is today. The last collision it experienced was massive enough to cause a chunk of the planet to fly off. This chunk didn't get very far, though. Instead, it got caught in the Earth's gravitational pull and started circling it. Thanks to this, it became the moon! When on Earth—again, pun intended—did all this happen, though? Time to play the guessing game! You know that the first elements started forming about 14 billion years ago and 380,000 years after the Big Bang (Warren, n.d.).

You also know that it must have taken a long time—the kind of long that puts car trips where you constantly ask, "Are we there yet?" to shame—for planetesimals to form, much less planets. So, when do you think the Earth and the moon officially formed? Take a guess:

_____

_____

Now, let's see if you've guessed right: The Earth and the Moon officially formed—drum roll, please—4.5 billion years ago! However, the Earth didn't look the way it does today when it first formed. Much like a Pokemon, it had to go through some evolution before it could take on its final form. What exactly did the earth look like, you ask? Well, when it initially came into being, it was absolutely covered in magma. So, it wasn't exactly a livable place, at least not if you dislike hot weather. Fortunately, all that magma cooled down bit by bit and, after a while, turned into rock and soil. Some magma remained in its core and still remains there today. That's why we have volcanic eruptions. While volcanic eruptions aren't fun to deal with, they were essential to the Earth after the magma on its surface cooled down. Each volcanic eruption, you see, releases a mass of gases, and these gases wove around the planet, mixing with some elements that were already there. In the process, they formed Earth's atmosphere, which allows us to breathe! Once Earth finally got its atmosphere, it developed its own climate and weather events. This allowed for water to form on the planet, and that, in turn, made life on Earth possible.

Alright, let's backtrack a bit. After all, that was quite a lot of information to lob at you, wasn't it? It might feel a little overwhelming to do all of this in one go. So, how about we map out all the events that took place and led to the creation of the Earth so that things become just a little easier to follow?

- In the beginning, the universe was just a very hot, dense dot.

- Then, the Big Bang occurred, releasing everything from that dot and sending it hurtling through space.

- As a result, the universe started growing, stretching, and expanding.

- At this point, the universe was way too hot for elements, even light, to form.

- However, things cooled down as the universe kept expanding.

- Once things got cool enough, the first elements, helium and hydrogen, were formed. They were soon joined by lithium and beryllium.

- By this time, the universe had cooled enough for light to form, too. We can still detect the light that formed then, using special devices, and this light is known as the cosmic microwave background.

- As things cooled down even more, the dust clouds that had been sending forth in the Big Bang and had been swirling all this time started forming into clumps.

- These clumps eventually grew into planets. Meanwhile, elements such as hydrogen and helium came together to form the first suns.

- These suns and planets came together as well, creating the first solar systems.

- Meanwhile, dying stars sent forth bundles of elements into the universe when they exploded, which ultimately played a part in the creation of new things like other planets and stars.

- As our solar system formed, the dust clouds gathered together to eventually form planet Earth.

- Planet Earth looked very different when it was first formed. It was covered in hot magma.

- The sun warmed Earth as it cooled over time. It also has its own atmosphere. This ensured breathable air existed on Earth and water could form on it, making Earth a livable planet.

Badabing, Badabang: Time to Draw the Big Bang

Now that we know the step-by-step process that followed the formation of, well, everything, here's a fun activity for you: Draw the Big Bang! Clearly, we can't travel back in time—yet—to observe what the Big Bang looked like. However, we can imagine it! So, what do you imagine the Big Bang looked like? How can one effectively depict the myriad of fascinating concepts that have been recently acquired? Ready? Set. Go!

Fun Fact: Did You Know You Were Star Dust?

Did you know that your body is actually made up of stardust? Yes, you are. So am I, and so is everyone you've ever met! OK, basic biology time: These tiny organisms, known as cells. Even tinier compounds, known as atoms, form these cells. The universe's building blocks are atoms, and stars created each and every one of them! Stars forge atoms and elements through a variety of chemical reactions at their cores. Then, a star explodes, unleashing those atoms and elements into the universe. These atoms travel far and wide, finding their way into planets like the Earth. On Earth, those elements and atoms come together to form... us! That means that you, my friend, aren't just the child of your parents. You're also the child of a star that exploded somewhere in the vast universe ages and ages ago!

Chapter 2:

Our Home, Earth

Did you know Earth is like a giant playground in space, filled with amazing adventures waiting for us to explore? Think about it: The universe is a massive place that only grows with each passing second.

It's home to about two trillion plants! However, as far as we know, the only planet in the universe with actual life is... Earth. Earth has enough oxygen for all living beings, like humans, to breathe. It is Earth that has enough water to keep all of us alive. It is Earth that has fast oceans, as well as vast deserts, lush green rainforests, fields of wildflowers, volcanoes, and so much more. Only the Earthllion has different creatures—from animals to humans and to insects—living on it.

How is all this possible? How did Earth become that one-in-a-billion planet where life could thrive? How can Earth be home to many environments, ecosystems, and creatures? How can all these creatures live in harmony—well, sort of—the way we do? If we want to unravel this mystery, we must understand the planet we call home a little better. We have to understand the delicate balance that makes all this and more possible. For this, we will have to go on an adventure. We will have to hop on our imaginary time machine and see how these different parts of the Earth came to be. Ready to put on your explorer's hat and join me on a journey across the globe? Well, then, let's go!

The Incredible Features of Earth

Imagine that you made a spaceship, Fineas and Pherb style, and decided to tour our solar system with it. You blasted off, and when you did, you saw that there are eight—or nine, according to some people who consider Pluto, a teeny tiny dwarf planet, to be an actual planet—planets in it. You landed on each of these planets, and while they were all really cool, you quickly realized something: Out of all of them, Earth is the only one home to any kind of life! This is what makes Earth really, really special. It's filled with people, animals, trees, insects, bacteria... Every corner of the planet is thriving with life.

So, why do you think this is the case? Why is Earth, out of all eight or nine planets in the solar system, the only one with life? There are many answers you can give to this question. So, if you answered, "because it's warm enough," you get a gold star. You also get a gold star if you say, "Because Earth has water," "We can breathe here," or "Because of...something to do with magnets." Well, you might only get half a gold star if you answered with that last one, but still.

Let's elaborate on our answers and discover why Earth is the ONLY planet to have all these things. Our first answer was that Earth is warm enough for life. The Earth is close enough to the sun to get enough heat. Of course, by close enough, I don't mean Earth is a stone's throw away from the sun. If that were the case, we'd all be like the Wicked Witch of the West, screaming that we're melting as we go about our days. Instead, I mean that Earth is 93 million miles away from the Sun (Greshko, 2018). "93 million? That's not close at all! That would take me 1,430,760 hours to drive!" I can hear you yelling, and wow! I didn't know you were such a math wiz! You're right, though. It would take you exactly that amount of time to drive to the sun if your car was space-worthy and going about 65 miles per hour. So, as the third planet from the sun, Earth isn't exactly the sun's next-door neighbor. However, given how hot the sun is, it is close enough to get all the heat it needs from it, thanks to the greenhouse effect.

Wait, Earth is warm enough for life because we built greenhouses on it? Not quite! Earth is warm enough for life because its atmosphere can trap enough heat from the sun—about 20% if you want to be exact. Earth's atmosphere comprises all sorts of gases, including carbon dioxide, methane, and water vapor. These gases are heat-trapping superheroes (*What Is the Greenhouse Effect?*, n.d.). So, they keep enough of the sun's heat and energy on Earth and make it possible for all sorts of things, like flowers and animals, and us to grow on it.

Earth's atmosphere isn't just good for turning up the heat. It's also essential for a little something called breathing. Unless you're a very specific type of parasite recently discovered, called hennuguya selminicola—try saying that as fast as you can five times in a row without messing up!—you need oxygen to breathe. All living creatures, except the bizarre hennuguya, do. Luckily for us, Earth's atmosphere has plenty of oxygen. Guess why! Go ahead; I'll wait:

You are correct if you talked about trees, forests, plants, or even algae in your guesses! All of these living beings perform a neat trick called photosynthesis. Have you ever watched Harry Potter? If you have, you've seen scenes where wizards and witches transform wood into metal and pocketwatches into mice. Well, photosynthesis is a bit like this, meaning plants and trees are like the wizards and witches of the natural world. This doesn't mean they can transform pocketwatches into mice, of course. Still, it does mean they can transform the carbon dioxide in the air into oxygen (Brown, 2024). That's what photosynthesis is all about!

So, Earth's plants, trees, and algae create all the oxygen we need to breathe. That oxygen is held on Earth by our handy, dandy atmosphere. But hang on... How can our atmosphere keep all the different gases in it on Earth? Why aren't those gases flying off into space? What a great question! Well, the short answer to it is "gravity." Earth, you see, has a lot of gravity. By that, I don't mean that the Earth is very serious, though some people on it can be. I mean that it has a gravitational pull. All planets have gravity. The greater the size and mass of a planet, the greater its gravity. Take Mars, for example. Mars is the fourth planet from the sun and is 1/100th the size of Earth (*Why Does the Atmosphere Not Drift off into Space?*, n.d.). Since it's tinier than Earth, its gravity is much weaker than Earth's, which means that, yes, you would be lighter if you weighed yourself on Mars than if you did so on Earth. However, you'd also have trouble breathing on Mars because its gravity is so light that a lot of the gases on the planet, like oxygen, fly off into space and go on discovery tours of their own. This doesn't happen to the Earth. Instead, our home planet's gravity keeps oxygen where we want it to be in our air and going in and out of our lungs.

There's another cool thing that our atmosphere does, other than keep us breathing it serves as a radiation shield. Fun fact: Sunlight has a ton of radiation, and radiation, as you may know, can be very bad for us. Imagine that we were creatures that didn't need to breathe and lived on a planet without an atmosphere. We'd survive without any issues, right? Not really, because then we'd be exposed to all that radiation coming at us from the sun. That radiation would make us sick, and we probably wouldn't be able to live for very long.

However, thanks to Earth's atmosphere and magnetic field, that's not a problem for us. Wait, magnetic field? What's that? Well, you see, the Earth is a bit like a massive peach, even bigger than the one in the book James and the Giant Peach. Similar to a peach, which boasts a large, ancient pit at its center, Earth also harbors a similar pit, formally known as its core. Molten iron constantly swirls around in Earth's core. This swirling motion creates a magnetic shield. If you're picturing the kind of bubble-esque shield you'd see around the Enterprise in Star Trek, you're on the right track. The only difference is that our magnetic shield is invisible. It doesn't protect Earth from missiles—not that there are any aliens throwing missiles at us, at least as far as we know.

There's one last reason why Earth has life on it, and that's because it has water. Did you know a human can only live three days without water? It's true. That's how badly our bodies need water. That's why doctors always go on about how you should be drinking water and not coke. Well, that is because Coke is very sugary, but you get the idea. As for why Earth has water and other planets like Mars don't... That's because the Earth is warm enough to have drinkable water. It's also because it has diverse enough weather for things like rain to take place, which refills the Earth's cups, meaning its lakes and stuff.

Fun With Earth's Forces

One of the most interesting things about Earth is that life takes on many forms here. There are plants, trees, humans, animals, and insects. There are also many different species of animals and even subspecies, to think about. Did you know, for instance, that there are a grand total of 1.2 million different animal species alone? How crazy is that? More importantly, how is this possible? How can Earth not only have plain, old life but also such a massive diversity of life?

Here's the thing: Earth is a bit like an experimental cook. I know that sounds weird, but bear with me! Imagine having a massive kitchen with lots and lots of ingredients to work with. You have everything from spices to vegetables, fruits, and different cuts of meat. That means that you have the opportunity to cook and bake all sorts of different dishes and desserts. You can experiment with ingredients all you want, too, and create unexpected, never-before-seen meals. Now, if Earth is our cook, it can do all this as well. The only difference is that Earth makes diverse and amazing new creations not with spices, vegetables, and the like but using different kinds of landscapes, climates, and ecosystems instead. How neat is that?

If oxygen, warmth, and water are the ingredients of life, then landscapes, climates, and ecosystems are the ingredients for having diversity in life. They're why we have all sorts of different creatures on Earth able to live in very different environments, like polar bears who hang out on the polar ice caps, cacti that can live in the desert, and tropical fish, which live in warm waters. But how did Earth end up with such varied landscapes, climates, and ecosystems? Wait, what are all these things, like ecosystems, anyway? Well, young padawan, let's find out!

Landscapes

Our first ingredient is landscape. So, how would you define a landscape? What do you think makes a landscape? Go ahead and try to write your own description for it:

Now let's see how you've done: Various landforms such as hills, mountains, sand dunes, fields, lakes, streams, plateaus, and more make up a landscape, which is a part of Earth's surface. All over the world, there are many different kinds of landscapes. The polar ice caps, for example, look nothing like the Sahara Dessert. The Sahara Desert is very different from the Amazon Rainforest. That rainforest looks nothing like the coral reefs in Australia or Mt. Everest. So, what makes all these landscapes different from one another? Why don't they all look the same? There are several reasons for this.

- climate

- geographical features

- human impact

Since we will discuss climate briefly, let's first explore the fascinating world of geographical features. Landscapes can be defined by numerous kinds of geographical features. Take mountains, for example. Mountains are majestic land features that rise toward the sky like they want to pierce it. Now, guess how mountains are formed! Surprisingly, the existence of mountains isn't thanks to weather events, though many other geographical features are. Instead, they form thanks to the movement of tectonic plates?

Tecto-what? Remember how we said that the core of Earth is basically molten iron? A vast amount of melted rock envelops that core. So, you know, it wrapped it in lava. Really thick and big bits of rock float on top of all that lava, and those things are called tectonic plates (Rutledge, McDaniel, Teng, Hall, et al., 2023). Tectonic plates are like the puzzle pieces that make up the world because entire continents rest on top of them, like sunbathers lying on pool floats. The pool floats they're on top of, then drift here and there. As they do, they sometimes knock against each other. This sometimes causes earthquakes. It also causes the landmass on top of our floaties and puzzle pieces to push and shove against one another, which makes all that rock and soil jut up and form mountains.

As you know, mountains have very pointy heads, steep sides, and slopes. If you've ever gone skiing, you'll probably be familiar with them. When it comes to skiing, snow often blankets the mountains because the temperature drops as you ascend, creating an ideal setting for sipping hot chocolate. Speaking of "hot," desserts are another common landform. They're very hot, arid, and sandy places, so that sand gets... everywhere! Here's an interesting fact that you might not know, though: Desserts are only hot during the day. At night, they're freezing cold instead! This bizarre situation arises because the desert lacks water and humidity. Desserts hardly ever get any rainfall, you see, which means there's no water vapor in the air to hold onto all that daytime heat.

Of course, the exact opposite is true for rainforests. That's why they have the word "rain" in their name. Rainforests are very hot and wet places, and they're as green as they can be. Did you know that 50% of all known plant and animal species live in the rainforests? How wild is that! It's almost as wild as the fact that most of the ingredients we use for lifesaving medicine come from rainforests!

Desserts and rainforests are two extreme examples of landscapes shaped by dramatic climates. In this sense, they can be considered the drama queens of Earth. Not all landscapes are quite so dramatic, of course. Some are much milder, and grasslands are a great example of this. Grasslands are like a halfway point between deserts and rainforests. They refer to vast stretches of grassy lands—who would have guessed—with some trees scattered here and there.

If there's one place that has even fewer trees than grasslands, it's tundras, which are found in polar regions. Polar regions are extremely cold places, in case the word "polar" didn't give that away. So, they're not great places to just chill—get it?—but they might be the best place to have a snowball fight, assuming you don't bother the polar bears.

So far, we've covered landforms that you're probably familiar with. So, here's a curveball for you: What do you think the Karst landscape is? Before you answer, these landscapes have nothing to do with cars. Any takers, then? No? In that case, Karst landscapes are things like caves, sinkholes, and disappearing rivers. Such landforms form when water erodes away rocks, such as limestone, that are a tiny bit soluble. Of course, they don't just form overnight. Instead, it takes many years— think centuries—for water to work magic, so you can go cave-spelunking.

Having mentioned water, we can't help but discuss aquatic landscapes. Aquatic landscapes include oceans and lakes, which make up about three-quarters of the Earth. That means that most of the Earth is actually made up of water. You heard that right! Here's some food for thought: 8.1 billion people live on Earth. Naturally, they only live on land since, unlike fish, humans can't breathe underwater. How many more people would there be on Earth, do you think, if there was less water and more land?

Then there are islands, which sort of "float" atop massive bodies of water, as you know. An island can be small or large, but it is always fully surrounded by water. They usually rise to the surface from the ocean floor after volcanic events—yikes!—or earthquakes, both of which shake things up enough for such a change to take place.

Last but not least, we have our built landscapes. Remember how we said that human impact is one of the reasons why we have different landscapes around the world? Well, built landscapes are the result of that impact. They're the cities where humans build the dams that they erect and more.

Climates

As you might have noticed, landscapes and climate have a very intimate relationship: The climate of a place helps shape its landscape, and the landscape helps determine the climate. Since we have such different landforms worldwide, we typically have different climates, too. Factors other than landforms, though, play a part in determining what the climate in a specific place will be like. What do you imagine those factors might be?

If you answered that question with the words latitude, elevation, and ocean currents, then bingo! You got it, right? If you didn't, that is perfectly fine. We're here to make all these exciting discoveries, after all. Let's kick off our first discovery with latitudes. Latitude refers to where exactly a place is on planet Earth. To understand why this affects the climate, we must travel back to outer space for a minute. You may remember from our earlier chapter that Earth revolves around the sun. It also revolves around itself like a disco ball.

On top of that, Earth tilts a bit to the side, much like the Tower of Pisa. As a result, the sun's rays hit different places on the Earth at different angles (Powys Whyte, 2024). The mid-drift of Earth, which we call the equator, receives more direct sunlight than other parts. So, the climate ends up being warmer at the equator. Meanwhile, the polar caps receive the least amount of direct sunlight. So, they end up being much, much colder!

That was simple enough, wasn't it? Then, how about elevation? Elevation refers to how high a place is on Earth. Remember how we said that the higher you go, the colder the weather gets when talking about mountains? This occurs due to the fact that ascending to a high altitude means escaping the heat that the atmosphere traps, particularly near the ground. The air gets very thin higher up, meaning that there aren't a lot of gases that can capture heat properly there. Hence, how high a place is plays a major role in how cold it ends up being.

Finally, we have ocean currents. What does the movement of ocean currents do with climate, though? After all, climate has to do with air and weather, and ocean currents occur in oceans. Well, you're correct in that the movement of ocean currents doesn't really affect climate. However, no matter how warm or cool those ocean currents are do. Places with warm ocean currents, as a rule, tend to have milder and warmer climates. Places with cooler currents tend to have cooler climates. Cool, huh?

Ecosystems

Earth has many different climates and landforms, as you saw. These climates and landscapes often come together in very unique combinations. Thus, these ingredients give rise to incredibly diverse dishes known as ecosystems. Pop quiz:

- What is an ecosystem?

- How do ecosystems work?

Since it is the world's easiest pop quiz, here are the answers to glance at before answering them! An ecosystem is a geographic region defined by a certain kind of landscape and climate and home to different animals, plants, and organisms with their own balanced circle of life, a la *Lion King*. The cool thing about ecosystems is that everything in this bubble of space affects another. For example, the temperature affects what kind of plants can grow there. The kinds of plants that grow there attract the animals that can eat them (Rutledge et al., 2023). The presence of these animals results in the presence of predators who can, in turn, munch on them. Those predators dissolve back into the Earth after they die and become food for the growing plants. Like I said, the cycle of life.

The thing about ecosystems is that they're delicate. Change one tiny thing within an ecosystem, and everything suddenly goes off balance, like a toppling Jenga tower. Suppose the temperatures in an ecosystem suddenly grow colder than are normal for the area. In that case, the plants there won't be able to survive. Once those plants die off, the animals that ate them won't have anything left to eat. So, they'll leave in search of food. When they do, the area's predators will have nothing to eat. As a result, they'll either have to leave or risk starving!

Time to Experiment!

Have you ever heard the saying, "All work and no play makes Jack a dull boy?" This saying is very true. So, now that we have learned all these neat things, it's time to play! In my experience, experimentation is one of the best ways to play. After all, you get to see so many cool things in experiments.

How to Turn Graham Cookies Into Mountains

Remember how we talked about mountains forming? Let's see how this happens with our own eyes, shall we? Of course, since we don't have the power to actually make tectonic plates move—assuming you're not one of the X-Men, that is—we're going to have to get a little creative. For this experiment, we're going to need (*Graham Cracker Plate Tectonics*, 2015):

- a box of graham crackers

- cool whip

- a plate

- a cup of water

Now, here's how you go about making Graham Cookie Mountain using all these things:

1. Take your plate and cover it with a cool whip. Make sure to spread the whip all over.

2. Put two graham crackers on top of your whip mantle. Make sure the two are touching.

3. Now, dip one end of your graham cookies in water, then put them back on the whip with their soggy sides touching one another.

4. Place your fingers on the dry ends of your graham crackers and gently push them toward one another.

5. Observe what happens!

Weather App Not Working? Build Your Own Barometer!

As you saw, different ecosystems have different climates, and these climates can all have very different temperatures, too. In fact, the temperature of an ecosystem can change day by day. So, how do you measure the temperature? I mean, without using your phone or computer to look it up? By building your own barometer, of course! How do you go about doing that? Well, first, you will need to get (Tammy, n.d.).

- a balloon (of all things)

- a glass jar

- a straw

- a thick, elastic band

- scissors

- some colorful pens

- some paper

- some tape

Have you gathered all your supplies together? Great! Now, let's begin:

1. Use your scissors to cut off your balloon's neck!

2. Take your jar and stretch your cut-off balloon over its open lid. Mind your fingers as you do this!

3. Place the elastic band around the lip of the jar to make sure the balloon stays in place.

4. Cut your straw at an angle so it has a pointy tip like a sword.

5. Place the straw on the balloon lid, with the non-pointy end at its center and the pointy end on the outside. The straw must be parallel to the ground. If it is, go ahead and tape it down in place.

6. Using your colorful pens, draw the sun on the top of your piece of paper and a rain cloud at the very bottom. Draw lines next to each symbol and one line right in the middle of them.

7. Place the jar and piece of paper near the window and watch what happens.

What will happen, then? Well, the air inside the jar will get heated or cooled depending on the temperatures outside. As a result, the balloon on the lid will expand or shrink! This will make your straw move up or down. So, on hot days, the pointy straw will rise closer to the sun. On cold days, however, it'll droop toward the rain!

My Very Own Ecosystem

Did you know that you actually build your own ecosystem? You can, no matter where you are, and pretty easily, too! All you need are (Butler, 2020)

- a glass jar

- some patches of moss

- a few small rocks

- some soil

You can gather all this stuff up by going for a little walk in a park nearby. Once you have everything, you can get to creating your ecosystem:

1. Hold your jar sideways and start by lining it up with the rocks you collected. This is important because rocks will keep excess water building in your jar and give the moss you'll add in something to cling to.

2. Next, get your hands a little dirty and add a layer of soil on top of your rocks.

3. Top your soil with damp moss. Dip the moss into water before placing the pieces in the jar. Try to get them to form a flat surface.

4. Now, close the jar's lid, seal it, and place it on the window sill in a sunny spot. Again, make sure it's sideways, as it lies there and doesn't roll off! It's good to like rock and all, but that's not the kind of rock and roll we want right now.

5. Sit back, relax, and observe. As the days go by, you'll get to watch your mini ecosystem's water cycle as drops form on its

top and rain back down, keeping the moss inside alive and thriving!

Design Your Own Planet

Now that you've explored the wonderful forces of the Earth, discovered how they worked, and even played around with them a bit, it's time for you to design your very own planet. You can design any kind of planet with any sort of climate, landscape, and ecosystem you'd like, so long as it's livable. This should be a piece of cake since you already know what a planet needs to have to be livable from the previous chapter.

Chapter 3:

The Sun and the Moon

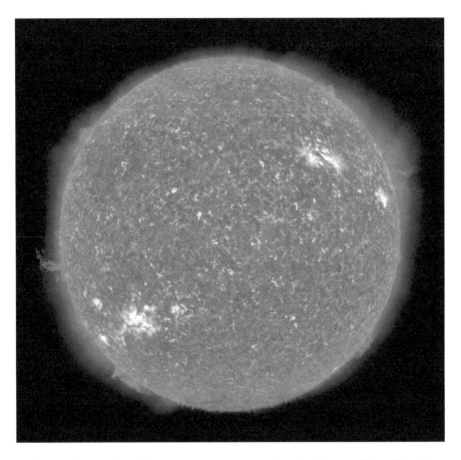

Did you know that the sun we see every day isn't actually yellow but white? It's true! It only looks like it's yellow because we see it through our atmosphere (Sukheja, 2022). As you can see, the sun consists of a multitude of colors. These colors all come together and appear white to us. The sun's rays break up our atmosphere as they pass through the air. Take a cup of water right now and put a pencil in it. Then, look at the pencil from outside the glass. When you do, you'll see that the pencil appears broken, even though it isn't. This is essentially what happens to sunlight as it passes through our atmosphere. In a unique way, this brokenness affects the color receptors in our eyes—the part of our eyes that allows us to see color. As a result, we see the sun in yellow. If we had a spaceship, we could take it to outer space, though. Since there is no air in space for sunlight to pass through and break up, we would see the sun as white.

How about the moon? Are there any fun, unexpected facts that you might never have heard of? Okay, here's one: Some people once believed that cheese, of all things, made up the moon. You know, the kind of cheese with holes you're used to seeing in cartoons? It's hard to say where this belief came from, but the saying that the moon is made of cheese is still around. Of course, by now, we know that the moon isn't made of cheese. The moon's composition mirrors that of Earth. This is because, as you'll recall, the moon used to be a part of Earth and split from it while going through its glow-up phase.

So, what other myths about the sun and the moon have we debunked over the years? What cool facts do we know about them? What is their relationship with Earth really like, and what more can we discover about them? It's time to find out!

The Sun, Our Greatest Ally

Earth has a very unique relationship with the sun. After all, thanks to the heat we get from the sun, there's life—like you and me—on Earth. Earth revolves around the sun, which is at the center of the solar system. The distance between the two is 93 million miles. Wait, I have a question: Why doesn't Earth fly away from the sun while it rotates? Why does it stick so "close" to it? Well, remember what we said about all planets having gravity? Well, the sun has gravity, too. Of course, you can't land on the sun to experience this gravity for yourself. You'd turn very crisp if you tried. But you actually experience it every day because the sun's gravitational pull keeps Earth going round and round in its orbit.

The sun is the main source of light and warmth on Earth. Without it, things would be very cold, very dark, and very, very lifeless. That's not a bad accomplishment for someone about five billion years old. You heard that right: Our good old sun is around five billion years old. It's a regular sun, much like our galaxy's 100 billion other suns (Turgeon & Morse, 2023). Like them, it was mainly made up of hydrogen and helium, which form what?... That's right; they form the core of stars or the sun, as they're the exact same thing. How exactly do stars form, though? How did ours form, for that matter?

Before our sun was the sun, it was just a cloud of hydrogen and helium molecules swirling about. Then, a supernova occurred nearby, sending shockwaves through space. These shockwaves flipped a switch for our cloud and triggered a chemical reaction between its particles. The energized particles began compressing like a bit of yarn would compress when you squish it in your hands. As this happened, the molecules started collapsing here and there, making them rotate and heat up. The more hydrogen and helium molecules did this; the hotter things became in this core until... boom! Nuclear fusion took place. Nuclear fusion occurs when two or more atomic nuclei—the cores of atoms, since everything seems to have a core—combine, creating a new, heavier element and releasing a ton of energy. Hence, the boom!

This chemical reaction and explosion then created the sun. So, the sun started giving off a lot of light and energy, eventually warming up Earth and allowing life to flourish. It might seem silly to some that the sun can do all this from 93 million miles away, but here's the thing: sunlight can travel a lot faster than any person, car, or even plane can. If you wanted to drive from the Earth to the sun, it would take you well over a million days, as you saw. It takes only 19 seconds for sunlight to travel that same distance!

Hang on a minute: How is it that the sun can actually warm Earth? Isn't it just a single star? It is, but it's a massive one! If you were to take the longest measuring tape in the world and measure the sun's radius— the distance from its very center to its edge—you'd discover that it amounts to 432,000 miles! That's 109 times as big as Earth! That's how ginormous the sun is! It's logical, then, that such a giant could create enough heat to keep us warm and happy, isn't it?

So, is the sun still made up of just hydrogen and helium? No, actually. Hydrogen and helium can still be found in the sun's core, but there are many more elements nowadays. There's nickel and oxygen, iron and silicon, sulfur, and magnesium. There's also calcium, neon, carbon, and chromium. However, these elements only make up a tiny portion of the sun—1.69% of it, to be exact. Meanwhile, hydrogen makes up three-quarters of the sun, and helium makes up the rest!

Fun fact: Did you know that the sun can actually conduct electricity? That is not something one would anticipate from a tremendous ball of fire, would it? This is because the sun has a magnetic field, and an electric current keeps running through it. How about this: Did you know that the sun rotates around itself like Earth does? What a copycat! Well, actually, Earth might be the real copycat here since the sun came first. Unlike Earth, though, the sun takes much longer to finish a single rotation. It takes Earth 24 hours to do a single pirouette. However, it takes the sun somewhere between 25 and 35 days to complete even a single turn! If living in the sun were possible, that'd be how long a single "day" would last.

Remember how we said that sunlight is a tad radioactive? Well, that means the sun itself is radioactive, too! That's why we must put on all that sunscreen when we go to the beach—to protect our skin from radioactivity. There are two types of radioactivity: X-ray and infrared, and the sun has them all. However, one of its primary radioactivity types is UV. UV is the only kind of radioactivity visible to the human eye because it contains all the colors in the universe. When all these colors come together, they appear to the human eye as white. However, our atmosphere breaks these colors apart as sunlight flows through it. So, we end up seeing the sun and sunlight as yellow! Because of this, scientists consider the sun to be the type of star known as a "yellow dwarf." I don't know about you, but that's the biggest dwarf I've ever heard of! I mean, Snow White's seven dwarves have nothing to do with the sun!

Just because the sun is a "yellow dwarf" for now doesn't mean it'll always be like that. At some point, the sun will change. This will happen when it consumes all the hydrogen that's within it. When that happens, its core will heat up even more, making the sun even bigger. How big will the sun get? It's hard to say exactly how big it'll be, but scientists assume its radius will be 200 times what it currently is! Wait... what does that mean for Earth? Honestly? We're not sure. We know that the sun will gobble up Mercury and Venus when it expands, but does that mean it'll eat up Earth, too? Well... it may. Alternatively, the sun's expansion might just push Earth farther away from it without eating it up. Let's hope the latter happens, though, rather than the former!

When the sun does expand, it will have turned from a yellow dwarf to a red giant. After that, it'll stay a red dwarf until it starts cooling! Over time, the sun's temperature will drop to around 180 degrees Fahrenheit. In the meantime, solar winds will kick up on the surface and continue until the sun's surface has completely cooled off. Only the sun's core will remain after that. Since that core will be white, the sun will have turned into a white dwarf.

Fortunately for us, this is a very long time away. Want to guess how long it'll be before the sun starts thinking about turning into a red giant? Go ahead! So, what was your guess? If you guessed a couple of hundreds or thousands of years... You got it wrong, I'm afraid. You also got it wrong if you guessed a few million years because the sun won't even be thinking about turning into a red giant until at least another seven or eight billion years have passed! So, it's safe to say we have nothing to fear, at least for now.

The Moon and Its Mysteries

Despite its lack of cheese-like qualities, the moon continues to captivate us. How could it not be when it is the first place in outer space, other than the Earth, that we humans have actually been to? With countless poems and songs dedicated to it, how could it not be? When you want to truly charm your crush, you should look up a poem about the moon the next time. You'll thank me later.

Anyway, the moon is basically a (massive) chunk of rock that used to be part of the Earth but got separated from it in a collision. It couldn't bear to be parted from Earth, though, so it remained in orbit. In other words, it got caught in Earth's gravitational pull and started circling it like a moth around a lit lightbulb. Hence, the moon is Earth's satellite. While the moon is smaller than Earth, it's not exactly small. For example, did you know that the moon is bigger than Pluto? That's part of the reason why Pluto got demoted from a planet to a dwarf planet!

How big is the moon, then? Well, the moon has a diameter of 2,159 miles, making it about one-fourth Earth's size. It orbits Earth, and the distance between the two is 238,860 miles. Here's a fun question for you: What would happen if the moon suddenly decided to crash into the Earth from that distance? Would it just leave a massive crater on Earth, or would it have more dramatic consequences? Here, why don't you write down what you think would happen in this situation:

_____

_____

Alright, let's see how well your imagination matches up with reality now. If something as big as the moon were to crash on Earth, I'm sorry to say that it would likely end all life on Earth. I'll tell you this: Remember the dinosaurs and how they went extinct? Well, the asteroid that caused them to go extinct was only 1/300th the size of the moon. So... that exactly bode well. Of course, the moon is a lot closer to Earth than that asteroid was. That means the moon won't be able to move at the same speed toward Earth as the asteroid did. It also means that, given how close the moon is to the Earth, it'll probably break apart in the Earth's atmosphere rather than land on the ground as a single, massive force. However, it would cause some dramatic changes on Earth, and those changes would sadly lead to our extinction.

OK, before you start worrying about this actually happening, let me put your mind at ease. There is little to no chance that the moon will crash land on Earth. In fact, there's more of a chance that the moon will eventually move very far away from Earth, like a good roommate parting ways with you, than that it will decide to cannonball to the ground. Why? Well, that's because scientists have discovered that the moon is moving farther and farther away from Earth every year! It moves 1.5 inches away from Earth every year, so it's possible that one day, many years from now, the two will actually part ways (Choi, 2017).

If they do, this will have some interesting consequences for Earth because the moon plays an important role in several things on Earth. For instance, the moon helps keep the Earth tilted at a specific angle. As you'll see in a bit, it plays a part in the seasons. It even helps control the tides in the ocean. If the moon were to suddenly disappear one night, we'd feel a terrifying jolt as the tilt of the world changed. We'd have a hard time figuring out what to do without tides, and it would take us some time to figure out how to manage our new seasons.

Luckily, the moon is in no hurry to move away from Earth. It's slowly drifting away, which means that any change that does happen once the two parts are combined will happen very slowly, giving us plenty of time to adjust.

The Seasons: The Great Contribution of the Moon

Wait, wait, wait... Hang on a second. What do you mean by the moon's effect on the seasons? Are you telling me that somehow the moon influences how hot the summer months are and how cold it gets in the winter? Well... No, not exactly. At least not directly. Here, I'll explain.

For this explanation, we're going to have to get a little numerical. We said that the moon affected the Earth's tilt a moment ago. The earth goes round and round on its axis, while the sun goes round and round, like a kind of solar merry-go-round. As the world turns, it tilts a bit to the side. In particular, it tilts its axis by 23.5 degrees (Gaughan, 2018). This affects how much sunlight falls over various parts of the world, affecting their climate and how the seasons play out there.

So, what does the moon have to do with all this? Well, like the Earth, the moon has its own gravitational pull. That means it gives the Earth just a tiny bit of a yank. This tiny yank proves enough to adjust the Earth's tilt. Without it, Earth would actually tilt at a larger angle. That would affect the way sunlight falls over different parts of the world, affecting the temperatures, and that would, in turn, influence... Drum roll, please... The seasons! Without the moon, seasons might look very different in different parts of the Earth! How different are we talking? That's a good question, and the answer is... We don't know! So, how about you imagine a world that's tilted at a different angle and what the seasons might look like there?

One of the cool things you may have noticed about the moon is its phases. Sometimes, you see a big, bright, full moon in the sky. Sometimes, it's a crescent moon that's giving you a wink. Some nights, the moon seems completely absent from the sky. Why is this the case? That's because the moon's light is actually light from the sun reflecting off the moon's surface. As the moon circles around the Earth and the sun, it keeps catching the light at different angles. Parts get a full blast of sunlight, while others get draped in darkness. Now that you know this, how about you get a telescope and observe the moon for a few nights? What phases can you catch it in? What does the crater-filled moon look like? Better yet, how about you draw your observations to really have fun with them:

We already asked what would happen if the moon decided to crashland on Earth out of the blue. So, here's another fun, though again outlandish, question for you: What would happen if the sun suddenly disappeared? Well, what do you think would happen?

Those are all excellent, very imaginative guesses. Now, let's see what the scientists have to say. If the sun were to suddenly wink out of existence...

- We wouldn't know about it for eight minutes (Hamer, 2019). That's how long it would take for the last dregs of sunlight to travel to Earth before a curtain of darkness suddenly fell over everything.

- Once everything became dark and nightlike, plants stopped photosynthesis. This would kill most plants and crops. Trees, however, would survive another decade or so because they are capable of going without sunlight for that long!

- A few days later, temperatures would drop low enough for the ocean's surface to freeze solid. Still, it would take a few thousand years for the oceans to completely freeze, so at least the cold-resistant fish would live a little longer.

- Finally, Earth's atmosphere would collapse, and cosmic radiation would find its way into Earth, making it completely uninhabitable!

Fortunately, this dramatic scenario will not play out for a very, very long time. We have a few billion years before anything close to this happens, so we have plenty of time to figure out what to do before then!

Chapter 4:

Fun Filled Tales of Space

Exploration

Did you know that your smartphone is millions of times more powerful than the computer that took astronauts to the moon? That's probably really surprising to hear. I mean, you use your smartphone to text, make phone calls, play games, and scroll on Instagram. Such things seem very unimpressive when you compare them to going to the moon, so how could a smartphone be more powerful than the computer that took us to space? Just because this is a surprising fact, though, doesn't mean it's not true. You see, man first set foot on the moon in 1969 during the Apollo Space Mission. Do me a favor: Google "Computers in 1969" and look at the images that pop up. Yes, computers really were that big back then. No, just because they were that big didn't make them more powerful. If anything, they were less powerful, which is what I said about your smartphone.

This begs the question: How on earth did we get to the moon with such bulky technology? For that matter, how is it that people looked up at the night sky, saw the moon, and immediately said, "I want to go there"? What did they do to make this happen, and what other great milestones did they reach in the meantime?

The Great Milestones of Space Exploration

When Americans first decided to go out into space, they didn't do it for the sake of exploration. They did it because this was a race, and they had to win it. No, seriously. This was literally a space race known as the Space Race, and its competitors were the USA and Soviet Russia. If you know a little history, you know that the U.S. and Soviet Russia didn't exactly get along. After World War II, things were especially tense between the two nations because the United States and Russia were basically on the brink of another war. The two world powers of the time frequently challenged one another and, unfortunately, had nukes. A lot of people were afraid that Russia would nuke America at some point and that America would retaliate or vice versa. People were so afraid of this, in fact, that they made instructional videos for schools, telling kids to duck under their desks if there was an attack. They assured children that ducking under their desks would protect them from nukes. As for whether they were telling the truth... If they were like Pinnochio, they'd walk around with the longest noses.

In any case, given how tense things were, Russia and the U.S. were frequently looking for ways to upgrade their missile technology. Specifically, they wanted to be able to shoot missiles from the comfort of their homes and even from space. To do this, they needed to be able to make ships or shuttles, as the U.S. would later call them, that could make it to space. So, the U.S. and Russia founded their space agencies,

NASA and Roscosmos, respectively, and got to work to make this happen. The race was on!

The space race wasn't originally about getting to the moon. It was about getting to space. It was Russia's Roscosmos that first managed to get to space. Have you ever heard of Sputnik? You might have. After all, Sputnik was the first satellite anyone has ever sent to space. Put in the Earth's orbit by Russia in 1957, Sputnik was the size of a beach ball. It was able to orbit the Earth in about 98 minutes and send the first message to Earth from space. What was that message? "Beep, beep, beep," of course. No, I'm not kidding. That was the actual first message.

In 1961, Russia also put the first man in space. Today, we call people who go into space astronauts, but did you know that Russia calls them cosmonauts? Well, Russia's first cosmonaut and the first man in space was Yuri Gagarin, who took a trip up to orbit in 1961. Gagarin stayed in space for 108 minutes (Nikola Sakay, 2021). Just 23 days later, NASA managed to send the first American man, that is to say, the first astronaut, into space. This man was Alan Shepard, though Shephard only stayed in space for about 15 minutes due to a technical glitch in his spacecraft! So, in a way, Alan Shepard put the "15" in "15 minutes of fame!" Joking aside, Shephard made it back to Earth safe and sound and became known as an American hero.

At some point, the goal of the space race changed. It turned from "go to space" to "land on the moon." Both the U.S. and Russia rolled up their sleeves and got to work, but in the end, the United States won! The U.S. managed to land two men on the moon, though they did send three over there. These three men were Neil Armstrong, Buzz Aldrin, and Michael Collins. It was Neil Armstrong, the mission's commander, who first landed on the moon, followed by Buzz Aldrin. Collins, however, didn't set foot on the moon. As the spacecraft pilot, he had to stay on board and ensure everything went well. He did have a fantastic view of the moon, though, and that's more than most people can say!

So, what do you think happened after that? Did the U.S. and Russia give up on space once the space race was won? Of course not! Would you give up on going to space once you'd figured out how? In some ways, getting to the moon was just the beginning of a new space exploration and discovery era. It also turned out to be the beginning of a new era of collaboration.

The new era of space exploration officially kicked off when NASA and Roscosmos said to themselves, "Hey, wouldn't it be really cool if we built our own stations in space?" So that's what they did. NASA and Roscosmos built their personal space stations in the Earth's orbit. NASA named its space station SkyLab. Russia named its own station Salyut 1. Eventually, things became much more friendly between the U.S. and Russia, so much so that U.S. astronauts and Russian cosmonauts of the Apollo and Soyuz crews shared an international handshake in space.

After the space handshake, the U.S. and Russia officially started working together on several space missions. These missions went so well that, at last, the two nations decided to merge their space stations to make one mega station. Figuring out how to merge the stations was a challenge. After all, they weren't exactly like Lego pieces that you could press together to make the Death Star, though that would have been very cool. Scientists spent many long hours figuring out which parts, nuts, and volts they had to add to which station so that the two could "dock" one another. The process of merging the stations started in 1998. Guess when it ended? Those are all very good guesses, but the real answer to that question was in 2011. So, did you get it right?

Once the stations had merged, the megastation they formed became known as the International Space Station (ISS). However, I maintain that the Death Star would still have been a cooler name. Over the years, many different nations' space agencies have added mini stations, known as modules, to the ISS. That means they've become partners with the station, started sending their own astronauts up to it, and really put the "international" in the "International Space Station."

The ISS currently consists of 16 different modules. Can you believe that that means the ISS is as big as an actual American football field? The ISS's massive size is beneficial as it ensures constant manned operations. That means there are always people on board. Can you imagine how annoying things would get if you didn't have some space on the ISS, especially since you can't exactly crack open a window or go for a walk—assuming you don't want to do a spacewalk—just to get away from others?

Does this imply that astronauts will permanently reside on the ISS? Actually, no! Only for a minimum of six months can astronauts reside in space. This is due to two things: radioactivity and microgravity. Remember how we said there's much cosmic radiation in space? Well, that much radiation can be very dangerous for people. Of course, protective materials cover the ISS to lessen that danger for astronauts.

Still, that protection can't protect them forever. So, astronauts have to come back down to Earth once in a while for the sake of their health and, you know, to see their families and stuff.

Astronauts also can't stay in space for long periods of time because of microgravity. You see, the ISS's gravity is so weak that it's called microgravity. On the ISS, astronauts basically float around because of it. When they go to sleep, they must strap themselves to their beds so they don't fly away and hit their heads while sleeping. They also have to use a suction cup-like device to go to the toilet so that their pee doesn't float away as they do their business!

Microgravity, as you can imagine, can lead to some very cool and funny situations. However, it can be problematic for astronauts' health, too. Here's why: When you're on Earth, your body has to constantly fight against gravity so that you can stay upright. Your muscles and bones constantly resist gravity, which makes you strong enough to walk, run, and jump. The ISS, however, doesn't have the same kind of gravity. So, your bones and muscles don't have the same kind of force to fight against. Because of this, they get much weaker in space, or at least they would have if astronauts hadn't worked out regularly on the ISS. By regularly, I mean every day, of course. As for how long astronauts have to work out to keep their muscles strong... that would be two hours a day, minimum! Yikes! Talk about how exhausted astronauts must get!

The ISS is still in the Earth's orbit, and astronaut crews regularly take turns living there. They conduct many cool experiments on the ISS and learn all sorts of things. However, the ISS isn't the only cool achievement mankind has made in space exploration. There are many more! For instance, in 1976, the U.S. sent the first-ever spacecraft, Viking 1, to Mars. They've since sent many landers and rovers to Mars, and these devices have gathered a lot of images and important information. However, they haven't discovered any Martians yet. The information gathered so far will be valuable when we land actual people on Mars, but more on that later!

Another really cool space exploration achievement was the Hubble Space Telescope. Did you know that Hubble was the first space telescope ever built? By "space" telescope, I mean that it's literally in space, by the way. It orbits the Earth from 340 miles away, which is why scientists can observe planets and galaxies that are millions of miles away from us. Who knows what type of discoveries Hubble will make over time? Maybe it'll discover city lights on another planet or spot the first-ever spaceship in space. The possibilities are endless!

Speaking of cool achievements, did you know that scientists can now land on comets? They did it in 2014. Scientists at the European Space Agency (ESA), a partner of the ISS, built a tiny robot they named Philae. I guess "Phill" seemed like a name that was too ordinary for this extraordinary robot. After all, Philae managed to travel to a comet about 316 million miles away from Earth! Philae was launched toward the comet in 1974, so it took nearly 30 years to get there. That's some road trip. Not only that, but Philae is still on this comet as it hurdles through space. I guess it'll still be with the comet, its new home, for many more years to come, assuming our unnamed comet doesn't find some new moon or planet to crash land on.

These are just some of the amazing accomplishments made in the age of space exploration. We have many, many more to look forward to. For starters, did you know that NASA intends not only to return to the moon in the next few years but also to build a lunar base there, similar to the ISS? That sounds like something straight out of a sci-fi movie! They're also planning to go to Mars in the 2030s, and by "go," I mean get people there. These people will be actual astronauts, of course, but who knows? Perhaps even tourists will be able to go to Mars in time. They can certainly go to space these days, so why not?

Oh, yeah, that's right. Space tourism is a thing now! You can actually hop on a spacecraft, like one built by SpaceX, and take a trip to low orbit. You can typically stay there for three whole days, so this might be a perfect long weekend getaway... if you have the money for it. Yeah, a trip to space is expensive. A single ticket currently costs $450,000 (Racine County Eye Staff, 2024)! So... maybe going somewhere more down to Earth might be a good idea. At least prices will come down, which they eventually will once space travel becomes a tad less expensive. Until then, if you want to travel to the moon, Mars, or space in general, you'll have to do it the old-fashioned way: By becoming an astronaut.

How to Become an Astronaut?

S121E06583

Becoming an astronaut is kind of a dream job. How could it not be? Very few people get to become astronauts and go to space, after all. This is because becoming an astronaut takes some hard work and time. For starters, you have to choose a scientific field to study. That's the thing: Most astronauts are scientists of some sort. They're engineers, chemists, physicians, mathematicians... They must be something of the sort because they must be capable of fixing things on their spacecraft, piloting them, and running all sorts of experiments in space. That's a large part of what astronauts do in space.

So, you start by choosing a science to study, and then you get to studying. That means you finish high school and go to university, where you continue studying something scientific. Oh, the horror! Once you graduate, you... do more studying because now, you'll have to get your master's and doctorate in your chosen scientific field. Only after you've gotten all those things will you be able to take the next step to becoming an astronaut, which is to take an exam by NASA to test your scientific knowledge. "Yay, exams! I love exams," said no one ever in the history of the universe. Still, you have to take and pass this one if you want to become an astronaut.

Passing this exam doesn't mean you get to become an astronaut immediately because you'll also have to prove you're physically and mentally fit for the job. For this, you're going to have to undergo some physical tests that will show (Tambe, 2023)

- you're a healthy weight and are physically in really good shape

- your blood pressure, blood sugar, and other such factors are good

- you maintain a balanced diet and workout regularly

- you have good eyesight and don't have any chronic health conditions

On top of all this, you must prove you have certain very specific skills. Fortunately, you can acquire most of these skills quickly if your goal is to become an astronaut. What exactly are these skills? Well, let's see:

- good communication skills and the ability to listen

- observational skills

- coordination

- teamwork

- leadership skills

- a high level of intelligence

- a high level of stamina

- curiosity

- resourcefulness

- adaptability

- ability to multitask

- patience and the ability to remain calm under pressure

- ability to trust

- a proficiency in English

So, what do you think? Do you think you have what it takes to become an astronaut? Will you diligently study and hone your skills to embark on thrilling space missions? If so, you may become one of the first people to ever set foot on Mars!

Big Question Time: When Will We Get to Mars?

So, will we ever get to go to Mars? Actually, yes, and much sooner than you think, too! NASA has been sending rovers, landers, and the like to Mars for many years, as you know. These machines have been gathering all sorts of data about the planet and what a trip there would actually take. Remember how we said that NASA was going to build a lunar base? Well, that lunar base will be up and running before the Martian missions begin. This is because the base will serve as a pitstop for astronauts on Mars.

With the technology NASA is developing, it turns out that getting to Mars will take nine whole months. Getting back from Mars is going to take about the same time. Add to that the days or weeks that astronauts will be staying on Mars and away from Earth for a year and a half. Astronauts can only spend that much time off Earth if they have the supplies they need. To ensure they do, NASA plans to send supplies to the lunar base ahead of astronauts. Astronauts will first head to the base and chill there for a few days. After catching their breath and picking up any extra supplies, they'll hop back into their spacecraft and head to Mars!

NASA has been planning its Martian missions for a long time. So long, in fact, that the woman who calculated the landing trajectories for the moon landing, Katherine Johnson, also calculated launch and landing trajectories for future Mars missions. This was back in 1969 with those ancient computers, mind you! So, you can imagine they must be updated a ton, but still! As for NASA's current plans, they intend to send just two astronauts to Mars, at least for that first trip. These two astronauts, who haven't been chosen yet, will stay 30 days on Mars! They will live in their spacecraft, which will be habitat-like. So, it's not like the astronauts will get to camp on Mars with actual tents. The idea might be tempting, but it would be pretty lethal if they tried. This is because Mars' air isn't exactly breathable for humans. How come? What makes Mars' atmosphere so different from that of Earth? What makes Mars so different in general? For that matter, how is Earth different from all the other planets in our solar system? Well, let's take a grand tour of our solar system in the next chapter and learn more!

Chapter 5:

Adventures in Our Solar System

Welcome, traveler, to our grand tour of the solar system! I'm your space travel guide, and I'm so excited to show you around. Now, I know you know a bit about our solar system already. You know, for example, that all the planets in our solar system revolve around surprise, surprise—the sun. You also know that Earth is the third planet from the sun, revolves around itself and the sun, and has a satellite called the moon. But wait... How many planets are there in the solar system? How exactly are they different from one another? Which one would be the most fun to visit?

My personal answer to that last question is Jupiter. This is because Jupiter is SO big that all the other planets in our solar system, including Earth, could fit in it! That's seven or eight if you count Pluto and the other planets! So, that means there are nine planets in our solar system. Those planets are Mercury, Venus, Earth, Mars, Jupiter, Saturn, Uranus, Neptune, and Pluto, because yes, I will count Pluto! After all, it is the farthest planet from the sun, which makes it rather unique, not to mention cold! What's the closest planet to the sun? Why? That would be Mercury. Things tend to get a tad sizzling there, as you might imagine, so you'd need buckets of sunscreen if it were possible to land there.

Here's a fun fact: Did you know that all the planets in our solar system, except Earth, were named after Roman gods? Really! Mercury, for example, was named after the Roman god of speed and money. I guess that makes it a rich planet. Meanwhile, Venus was named after the Roman goddess of love, and Mars was named after the god of war. Saturn, meanwhile, was named after the god of time, and Uranus after the god of the sky. Last but not least, Pluto was named after the god of riches, so perhaps that's the actually wealthy planet despite its small size. Well, you know what they are: Size doesn't actually matter!

What about Earth, then? What was it named after... I hate to break to you, but Earth wasn't named after cool deities like the other planets because the word Earth literally means "ground." So, whoever named Earth called it the ground and left it at that. As for who that person is, we don't actually know. We only know that they weren't the most imaginative. How about you, then? If given the opportunity, what name would you have given to the Earth?

The Planets of Our Solar System

Since we've already spent a lot of time focusing on Earth, let's focus on the eight other planets in our solar system. Did you know, for example, that you can divide the planets into two categories: terrestrials and gas giants? Wait, terrestrial? As in extraterrestrial? As in aliens? Does that mean some of our solar system's planets have aliens on them?

Well, no. At least, not that we know of. The word "terrestrial" doesn't mean "aliens," you see. Instead, it means "rocky" (Dutfield & Gammon, 2019). Scientists describe certain planets as "terrestrial" planets rather than as rocky planets because, as anyone who has ever studied science knows, scientists like giving long, complicated-sounding words to things. I imagine they have a meeting about naming things, where they try to come up with as weird-sounding names as possible. I'd love to peek in if they do, but I digress.

So, terrestrial planets mean rocky planets. This doesn't mean that they have a rocky surface. Rather, "rockiness" refers to the planets' cores. You see, terrestrial planets have cores made of molten rock and iron. Earth fits this definition, as we have already seen. So do three other planets: Mercury, Venus, and Mars. What about gas giant planets, then? Well, those are planets mostly composed of gases like hydrogen and helium. Jupiter, Saturn, Neptune, and Uranus fit this description perfectly! Wait, but what about Pluto? Is it a terrestrial or gas-giant planet?

Actually, Pluto is neither. Pluto is the farthest planet from the sun, as you know. So it's very, very cold. Pluto is so frigid that ice makes up the majority of its surface. Since Pluto is an exception to most of our solar system's "rules," let's start our grand tour of the solar system with it and work our way inward. So, we already know Pluto is very small, but how small are we really talking about? If you want specifics, Pluto is about 1,400 miles wide. That means that it's about half the size of the United States! Yes, there is actually a planet as tiny as that! That's why we previously referred to it as a dwarf planet.

Another fact you already know about Pluto is that it's the farthest planet from the sun. So, how far away is it, really? 3.6 billion miles, to be exact! That's why it's -387 degrees on Pluto! The planet is so far away that sunlight can barely reach and warm it up (*Pluto: Facts*, 2023).

So, you already knew some of this about Pluto. How about some things you might not have known? For instance, did you know Pluto has not one, not two, or three, but five whole moons? All of these moons are smaller than Pluto itself, of course. The largest one, Charon, is only half Pluto's size! Given those proportions, some scientists don't really consider Charon a moon. Instead, they treat Charon and Plato as double planets that circle around one another like dancers. What do you think, then? Do you think Charon should be considered a moon or that it could be considered Pluto's companion planet?

Let's imagine we somehow managed to get our hands on thick enough coats to keep us warm on Pluto, and we decided to land and take a walking tour of the planet. How long do you think that day will last? Before you answer that question, remember: Since Pluto is the farther planet from the sun, it has the longest orbit to follow around the sun.

It takes Pluto 248 years—yes, years, not days—to complete a single orbit around the sun. So, time flows much more slowly on this planet. So, how long did you guess a single day on Pluto would last? If you replied to that question within 153 hours, congratulations! You were in the right ballpark!

Now that we've taken a tour of Pluto and seen that there isn't much to see on it except ice, ice, and more ice, let's hop back on the space bus and go somewhere just a little warmer: Neptune. Neptune is a brilliant blue planet. The Roman god of the sea inspired the name of Neptune. Neptune, the eighth planet from the sun, is a cold place, though it is a little warmer than Pluto. Neptune's biggest tourist attraction isn't its ski slopes, though. They're the planet's supersonic winds. Sonic winds are incredibly fast, just like Sonic the Hedgehog, which is as blue as Neptune if you haven't noticed. In fact, the winds on Neptune are the fastest in our solar system. So, they'd be great for kite surfing if, you know, we could survive them.

Like Pluto, Neptune takes a while to orbit around the sun. It takes Neptune 165 years to do so (*Neptune: Facts*, 2023). In 2011, the planet actually completed its first orbit since its discovery in 1846. Unlike Pluto, however, Neptune is quite a big planet. Its diameter is 30,775 miles, meaning it's four times as wide as Earth. Despite its size, days here are shorter than on Earth. A day on Earth lasts 24 hours, but on Neptune, a single day ends in 16 hours!

Like many planets, Neptune has its own moons. Care to guess how many moons it has? Hint: It's more than Pluto does. As far as we know, Neptune has a whopping 16 moons in all! The largest of those moons is Triton. It's not Triton's size that makes it unique among all the moons in our solar system, though. It's the fact that it goes in the exact opposite direction that the planet rotates, as it orbits Neptune. So, if Neptune turns clockwise as it rotates, Triton goes counterclockwise like an unruly child. Why might that be? Scientists have a few ideas, but they don't yet know. So, go on. Make a wild guess:

A number of scientists believe that Triton wasn't originally one of Neptune's moons. It was just a passerby on its way somewhere else. However, it got caught in Neptune's gravitational pull and got stuck in its orbit, or so their logic goes. If that truly is the case, I wonder where TriEarthame is from on Earth?

Neptune doesn't just have a lot of moons. It also has five rings and four ring arcs. So, I'm a big fan of the song "Put a Ring On It." Dust, ice, and dark matter make up Neptune's rings. Scientists believe that various collisions with the planet created the rings. Scientists believe that the planet originated approximately 4 billion years ago. Neptune, being an ice planet, has layers of ice, water, ammonia, and methane. There may be some boiling hot water on its surface, too, though we don't know for sure since we can't get a close enough look to check... yet.

Now, onto the seventh planet from the sun: Uranus. Uranus is a bit of an oddball, as it likes to spin sideways as it goes around the sun. With a diameter of 31,763 miles, it's the third largest planet in our solar system and, like Neptune, has a lot of rings. At first glance, you might think that Uranus is an ocean planet, thanks to its blue-green color. It owes its pretty color to methane, though, as there's a lot of it on the planet. So, going swimming on Uranus is probably not the best idea, and neither is breathing without an oxygen tank.

Here's an unexpected fact for you: Did you know that Uranus has the coldest atmosphere out of all the planets in our solar system? Wait, that can't be possible! After all, Uranus isn't the farthest planet from the sun; Pluto is. I assure you, it is possible. You see, most planets have big and warm cores that keep them relatively warm (Choi, 2017b). Uranus' core, however, is pretty small. So, it can't warm up properly from the inside out, even if the planet does get a bit more heat from the sun compared to Neptune and Pluto.

Let's see... What else do we know about Uranus? Honestly? Not much! This is because we haven't been able to send any rovers or anything like that to Uranus yet. One day, however, we will! In fact, NASA plans to plan missions for Uranus in the coming years. So, who knows? Perhaps we'll get some exciting new developments very soon!

We might know relatively little about Uranus, but we know a lot more about Saturn, our second-largest planet and the sixth from the sun. After all, it's the ring-iest planet in our solar system, so it has been a bit of a fascination since its discovery (Choi, 2019). Unlike other ringed planets, Saturn's rings are pretty icy. Saturn has the honor of being the farthest planet from the Earth to be discovered without a telescope. It was the gold, old human eye that first spotted Saturn and all the way back in ancient times, too! However, when first spotted, it must have had impressive eyesight!

Of course, looking at Saturn through a telescope is a lot more fun than squinting at the sky. That's when you can actually make out its rings, after all. It's when you truly get to behold its size as well. After all,

Saturn is nine times as big as Earth! The most surprising thing about Saturn, however, is that it can float! Wait, what? OK, imagine that you had a shrink ray and that you pointed it at Saturn and fired. Saturn shrank to the size of a baseball, and you plucked it up the same way Gru did to the moon in *Despicable Me*, except without the minions. Then, for some reason, you brought Saturn to your bathroom and filled your tub with water. You then chucked Saturn in. If you were actually able to do that, or, alternatively, make a bathtub large enough to fit Saturn into its original size, Saturn would float in the water! This is because Saturn has a lower density than water!

If you're done playing around with your shrink ray, we can move onto the fifth planet from the sun, Jupiter. If you're wondering what the biggest, fattest planet in our solar system is, look no further than Jupiter (*Jupiter*, n.d.). That's probably not surprising, though, seeing as we already set it to fit all other planets in the solar system inside itself! A lot of people look at Jupiter and think that its ground must be red and brown because it's covered in red and brown stripes. The truth is, however, that those stripes aren't Jupiter's soil. They're its clouds. Jupiter even has a massive red birthmark that isn't crater-like, some people think, but the massive storm that has been raging for hundreds of years! When I say massive, I mean that that storm is as big as the Earth! It makes sense now that Jupiter was named after the Roman god of the sky, doesn't it?

As interesting as all these planets in our solar system are, the one we know most about—apart from Earth, obviously—is the fourth planet from the sun: Mars. How can that not be the case when it's our next space destination after the moon? Mars is just a little smaller than the Earth, as its diameter is 4,220 miles. Since it is smaller than Earth, its gravity is less powerful as well. Say that you weigh 100 lbs. on Earth (*Planet Mars*, 2019). If you were to bring a scale with you to Mars and weigh yourself there, your new weight would be 38 lbs! So, you don't have to go on a diet to lose weight, it seems. You just need to go to Mars.

Mars is a bit of a slowpoke since it takes 687 days to go around the sun. A day on Mars, though, is only 37 minutes longer than one on Earth, so go figure! The planet is significantly warmer than Pluto, but it isn't exactly a tropical island. I mean, the average temperature on the red planet—and believe me, it's very red—is -51 degrees Fahrenheit. Still, that's a great deal more survivable than some of the other planets in our system, at least so long as you wrap up warmly. Mars has two moons that keep circling around it. The Greek gods named them Phobos and Deimos.

This is weird. Why are all planets named after Greek and Roman Gods? Well, because most of them were discovered by the ancient Greeks. They believed that gods watched over them. It seemed logical to them that the weird things they saw up in the night sky, like a red star, which is what Mars looks like to the naked eye, would be those gods. The Roman Empire that came after them agreed with this thought. They didn't, however, want to use the Greek names for Gods. So, they just went with Roman ones instead. The ancient Greeks and Romans established a trend that scientists and astronomers later adopted, naming planets and moons after various gods and goddesses.

Going back to Mars, here's one last fun fact about it: Mars is a very dusty place. You know Mars is called the red planet? That's partly because a lot of dust storms take place on Mars, and these storms can last a long time. By "long," I mean for a few months! Still, storms that last a few years sound better than ones that last for years, like the one on Jupiter, right?

Mars, as you know, is the planet that we human beings aim to head to next. This isn't because Mars is the closest planet to us. It's because it's the planet on which we stand the most chance of surviving. All we have to figure out is how to live in its temperatures, deal with its dust storms, and breathe in its air. Mars has very little oxygen in its atmosphere. In fact, carbon dioxide makes up 96% of the atmosphere. We're not plants, so that's not really breathable for us, which means we really have to put our thinking caps on before we head to the red planet!

If Mars isn't the closest planet to Earth, what is? That planet would be Mercury, which is also the second-smallest planet, after Pluto, to dwarf a planet in our solar system. Mercury, a gray planet teeming with numerous planets, bears a striking resemblance to the moon. That's a nice coincidence since it's only a bit bigger than the moon. Mercury is the first planet from the sun. That means that the sun would appear three times brighter on Mercury than it does on Earth, and eleven times brighter! I wonder what kind of extra-special sunglasses you'd need so you can walk around without your eyes watering all the time?

Hang on a moment... How can Mercury be the closest planet to Earth if it's the first planet from the sun? Shouldn't the closest planet to Earth be Venus, which is the second planet from the sun? Well, the reason for this has to do with the planets' orbits. You see, Mercury and Earth are often on the same sides as they orbit the sun. Venus, on the other hand, often falls on the opposite side of the sun than the Earth, as the planets orbit it. So, Mercury ends up being closer to Earth than Venus does!

Speaking of orbits, did you know that Mercury is like the solar system's flash? This planet is so fast that a single year on it lasts only 88 days! The Roman god of speed inspired its name. Personally, I might have named it after Speedy Gonzales, but oh well! Still, that doesn't mean I'd want to go there since I'm not a big fan of beyond-boiling-hot weather. That's not an exaggeration because the average temperature on Mercury is 840 degrees Fahrenheit! Nights on Mercury are a little more bearable, though. They're typically a balmy 275 degrees Fahrenheit (Choi & Dobrijevic, 2017). Of course, there are parts of Mercury that are actually cold. That's why NASA was able to find some ice in the craters found at Mercury's southern and northern poles.

Did you know that Mercury is the only planet that we know of that continually shrinks? Really! You see, Mercury has an iron core that cools bit by bit with every passing year. As it cools, this molten iron core solidifies, and as it solidifies, its size shrinks! I wonder how tiny Mercury will get when its core fully solidifies. Only time will tell, I suppose!

Our last planet is Venus, which is the second planet from the sun and the hottest planet in our system. Question: Why do you think Venus is the hottest planet in our system despite being the second planet from the sun? Go on! Give me your best guess:

———————————————————————————————

———————————————————————————————

Alright, now let's see how close you got. The reason Venus is the hottest planet is... because of its atmosphere. Venus's atmosphere has a lot of greenhouse gases. Specifically, it has a lot of carbon dioxide. As we know, these gases are great for holding on to the heat of the sun. On Earth, they make things warm enough for there to be life. On Venus, they make it hot for there to be life! Not only that, but Venus' atmosphere is so thick that if you were to land on it, the sun would look like nothing more than a blurry spot to you before you burned up, I mean! Things can get as hot as 900 degrees Fahrenheit on Venus, you see.

Venus is home to one very weird phenomenon: Dark streaks frequently appear on the planet and stay there regardless of the weather. Scientists have no clue, so far, why these streaks appear and how they're able to withstand hurricane-strength winds (*Venus: Facts*, 2024). They also have no idea why these streaks are able to absorb ultraviolet radiation. They do have a theory, though, which is that these streaks are made of really thin ice particles. Some scientists also think that there might be some form of microbial life that we're unfamiliar with. As for which scientists, if any, are right, that's going to be tough to figure out. We likely won't be able to until we're able to create some kind of spacecraft that can land on Venus without melting.

Once we do manage to land on Venus, we'll have plenty to explore since it's about the same size as Earth. However, Venus can be considered more similar to the moon because, like the moon, it has phases. That means that Venus sometimes looks to us like a crescent and sometimes like a half-planet, as opposed to a half-moon. Try to watch the different phases of Venus if you ever get your hands on a telescope. Better yet, try to record them the way you did with the moon. Don't forget to have plenty of red and orange markers as you do this since Venus looks like it has been painted in those colors.

Out of all the planets in our system, Venus has to be the slowest. Can you believe that a single "day" on Venus takes 243 Earth days? Funnily enough, a year on Venus is actually shorter than a day on it! That means that it takes Venus less time to do a full orbit around the sun than it takes for it to do a full orbit around itself! A year on Venus, therefore, lasts just 225 days! How crazy is that?

The Mysterious Planet 9

We're used to thinking that our solar system is only made up of eight planets, excluding Pluto. However, that might not really be the case. We might, in fact, have a mysterious ninth planet in our midst that we know little to nothing about! Far away in the distance, way past Neptune and Pluto, are a cluster of small space objects. Scientists call these things trans-Neptunian Objects because, again, they are like giving things hard-to-pronounce names. Luckily, they're all right with shortening this name to TNO. Anyway, these TNOs bunch together and spin around themselves like planets do. However, they seem to be spinning away from other planets rather than around our sun. There can only be one reason these TNOs aren't being pulled toward the sun thanks to its gravity: They're caught in the gravitational pull of some other space object big enough to attract them.

What object, though? That's the question! Scientists believe that this object can be one of two things. First, it might be another massive planet that's 10 to 20 times the size of the Earth to have such an effect (Rafi Letzter, 2019). Second, it might be a primordial black hole! What is that? Is that a fancy word for a regular black hole? No, actually. A primordial black hole is a bit different from a regular black hole. A regular black hole is something that forms after a star collapses and that sucks in everything that's around it, even light. Sucks into where? Good question, but we don't know! We've never been inside a black hole before because if we did go into it, we'd never be able to get out. Also, we've never been able to get close enough to one, so there's that.

What makes a primordial black hole different from a regular one, then? Well, a primordial black hole doesn't form from a collapsed star. Instead, it forms in really dense parts of the universe. Dense with what? Forms how? I have three words for you: We don't know. But who knows? Maybe we'll be able to find out if we can locate the mysterious Planet 9 and see if it's an actual planet or a primordial black hole like some think.

Cosmic Architect: Make Your Own Solar System

We've read several interesting things about the solar system. Now, let's interrupt our reading session and get our hands dirty by building a model of our solar system! Here's what you're going to need for this crafty arts-and-crafts project:

- a large foam ball

- nine smaller foam balls of different sizes

- construction paper

- glue

- a foam platform

- skewer sticks

- paint and paintbrushes

Start by skewering the largest foam ball and painting it yellow. This will be your sun. Now, skewer it in place on the center of your foam platform. That done, skewer all your balls—I mean, planets—and paint them according to which planet they are. Be careful to choose the smallest ball for the smallest planet and the biggest one for the biggest planet.

While your balls dry, cut some rings out of your construction paper for your ringed planets. Once the paint is dry, glue them in place. Finally, fix all your planets into place with your skewer sticks.

Hang on a minute. This model is pretty stationary, isn't it? Aren't planets supposed to move about? Yes, they are. So, how can you make a model with moving planets? How about you come up with an idea or two for this one? Here, I'll give you some hints: You'll need some string and a large enough cardboard box.

Big Question Time: How Did the Solar System Form?

So, we know how Earth formed. We know how the sun came to be. Based on all that you've learned, how do you think our solar system itself form? Oh, I have an idea! How about we madlib this:

Our solar system formed _____ years ago. Initially, it was a big cloud of _____. Then, this cloud collapsed after feeling the shockwaves created by a nearby _____, which is an exploding star. The impact created a reaction between the hydrogen and helium particles at the center of the cloud, which came to form _____. After the sun formed, its _____ drew the various objects around it toward itself. These objects were particles that clumped together and collided with each other as they moved and they came to form _____ like Earth. Some pieces broke off from these planets but were still caught up in those planets' orbits. These became their _____. So, the planets and their moons kept circling the sun, always following the same paths, which are known as their _____.

Chapter 6:

Milky Way Marvels and Galactic Surprises

Our galaxy, the Milky Way, does not consist of milk, just as the moon does not. So why is it named the Milky Way, and why are scientists so obsessed with dairy? Are they all lactose-intolerant or something? Well, I don't know about lactose intolerance. However, I am aware that the Milky Way earned its name because, when viewed through a telescope, it resembles a band of milk spilled over a very dark patch of space. The Ancient Greeks used to think that the Goddess Hera, not a wayward cat as some may think, was the one who spilled that milk, by the way!

Thus, it appears that they genuinely believed that the Milky Way formed the galaxy. Go figure!

The Milky Way may not be made of milk, but it is made of many solar systems, planets, suns, and other wonders. What's more, it only keeps gathering up more space wonders as time passes. This is because the Milky Way is, well, a cannibalistic galaxy. You see, it has a tendency to eat other galaxies. No, that does not mean the Milky Way has teeth, though that would be something to see. It just means that the Milky Way keeps colliding with other galaxies and absorbing them into itself. In fact, it's in the process of doing that at this very moment. Scientists have recently told us that the Milky Way is munching on the Sagittarius Dwarf Spheroidal Galaxy (Young, 2021). Well, then, bon appetit!

How big is the Milky Way, then? Simply put, this galaxy is big enough that traveling from one end to the other would take you 25,000 years to reach, and that's if you could go at lightspeed (Dalcanton, 2012). That's a shame! It means we won't be able to tour the Milky Way in spaceships just yet. However, just because we can't tour it doesn't mean we can't explore it using advanced telescopes, scanners, and other cool pieces of technology. With that in mind, what have we learned about the Milky Way so far? What secrets have we uncovered, and what mysteries do we still want to reveal? Let's find out.

The Milky Way Unveiled

First things first: The Milky Way is a spiral galaxy. That's because if you were able to look at it from above or below, you'd see that it resembles a spinning pinwheel a bit. Except, of course, that it's a lot prettier than that. Our solar system is located on one arm of this spiraling galaxy. Other stars contain many other solar systems and celestial surprises.

Think about all the stars you can see at night. Let me rephrase that: Think about all the stars you would be able to see if there wasn't any light pollution preventing you from doing so. In this case, you would be able to see 6,000 different stars without using a telescope. That's a lot of stars, to be sure, but they're only a tiny fraction of what the Milky

Way contains. That being the case, guess how many stars are in the Milky Way!

If you guessed something close to 100 billion, congratulations! You're on the right track. However, stars are not the only components of the galaxy. Dark matter actually makes up most of the Milky Way. I mean that 90% of the galaxy is dark matter (Couture, 2015). For the record, dark matter refers to material that is not visible. What about the visible elements, such as stars? Are they actually called "light matter"? Well, yes, sort of. Specifically, we refer to them as luminous matter, a term that, let's admit, carries a more poetic connotation than dark matter. How do we know that dark matter is there if we can't see it?

Again, great question! We know that dark matter exists because the Milky Way likes to spin like everything else in space. Scientists have figured out how to calculate how fast the Milky Way spins. In doing so, they realized that the stars in the galaxy would be spinning and moving at much lower speeds if dark matter didn't exist. As for the luminous matter, it's not just made up of stars. About 15% of luminous matter is gas and stardust. On very clear nights when there's no light pollution, you can see this dust in the sky. It looks like sparkling white dust has been sprinkled across the night sky.

Here's a question for you: What's in the center of the Milky Way? Is it another sun, do you think, or something entirely else? Actually, the thing at the Milky Way's center is a supermassive black hole! This black hole even has a name: Sagittarius A. It is absolutely gigantic, with a diameter that's 14 million miles long! Could you envision yourself engulfed in such a vast expanse? What would happen to you if you truly fell into it?

OK, if you were to fall into Sagittarius A specifically, one of two things would happen to you. First, you might be stuck forever and ever inside that black hole. After all, there is nothing that would be able to counter its gravitational pull and get you out. That is unless there was a back door. That brings me to the second thing that might happen to you inside Sagittarius A: This black hole might just spit you out somewhere else in the galaxy or even the universe! Scientists believe that black holes are connected to white holes in other parts of the universe. Black holes, they say, suck things in, while white holes spit things out

(Freeman, n.d.). Has this theory been proven yet? Well, no, because no one has been inside a black hole—at least not one that we know of! However, we've seen plenty of movies testing the theory, so who knows? Maybe astronauts will run a bold experiment in the years to come to see if they end up somewhere else or get spaghettified!

Oh, right! That's the second thing that could happen to you in a black hole: You might get spaghettified, depending on what kind of black hole you fall into. Yes, that's an actual word! You see, some black holes' gravitation pull is so strong that, if you were to fall into one, your body would be stretched until it looked like very thin and very long spaghetti. That... doesn't sound like a pleasant experience at all. So, maybe let's just avoid that!

So, then, what else do we know about the Milky Way, then? We know, for instance, that the Milky Way is almost as old as the universe itself! The universe, you see, is about 13.7 billion years old. How old do you think the Milky Way might be? Any guesses? Well, the Milky Way is... precisely 13.6 billion years old! So, the universe is only a hundred million years older than it! Of course, parts of the Milky Way are "newer" than other bits. After all, the Milky Way keeps consuming other galaxies. How could that be the case, though? How could the Milky Way possibly be eating things up?

The Milky Way can gobble up other galaxies because it's constantly moving! Is that really all that surprising, though? So far, we've seen that planets, suns, moons, and solar systems cannot sit still for a moment. Why should the galaxy be able to? How does the Milky Way move, then? It spins around, a la pinwheel, to be sure, but that's not all. The Milky Way also cruises through space. I do actually mean that it cruises because, at present, it's moving in a single direction and going 1.3 million miles an hour. As it does, it keeps coming across other galaxies and gulping them all down. By that, I mean that it makes them a part of itself, especially if they happen to be smaller than it. Wild, right?

Our Galactic Neighbors

As you can gather from all that, the Milky Way isn't the only galaxy in the universe. There are many others, some of whom are our as-yet-uneaten neighbors. Scientists believe that there are between 100 and 200 billion galaxies in the universe! Sadly, we haven't been able to count them all but one day! We have been able to count the ones in our neighborhood, though. OK, to be clear, we're not too close to the neighbors in our neighborhood. They typically live about 10 million light years away from us. Still, that's close enough to watch them through telescopes, count them, and give them a wave. At last count, there were—drumroll, please—50 galactic neighbors in our neighborhood.

Scientists called our neighborhood the Local Group. That sounds like a WhatsApp chat group, doesn't it? Our closest galactic neighbor in this chat group is the Large Magellanic Cloud. The Large Magellanic Cloud (LMC) also happens to be our largest neighbor. It's so large, in fact, that you can actually see it in the sky if you're in the southern hemisphere and somewhere where there's no light pollution. As large as LMC is, though, it's still a dwarf galaxy. If it were to ever collide with the Milky Way, it would likely be absorbed by it. Fortunately for it, there's no chance of that happening, at least so far. LMC is a good 161,663 lightyears away, after all.

Did you know that the LMC isn't just a dwarf galaxy but also an irregular galaxy? Hold on! What's an irregular galaxy? An irregular galaxy is one that looks like a spiral, similar to the Milky Way, but has an off-center bar running through it. This arm has a disjointed spiral that sprouts from it as well, which means that this type of galaxy is quite uniquely shaped or, you know, irregularly shaped. Hence, the name.

Why the bizarre shape? There are a number of theories about this, but before that, why do you think this might be the case? Go on, write down what you think, and share your thoughts:

What an interesting idea! Now, let's see how it holds up to what the scientists have theorized. Most scientists think that LMC's shape is thanks to its interactions with the Milky Way's gravitational pull, which

LMC can feel from even that distance. I guess you can say that LMC is as sensitive as the princess from the Princess and the Pea. Scientists also think that LMC's shape got distorted because the Milky Way has a dark matter halo with which the dwarf galaxy has been interacting. Of course, the Milky Way might not be to blame for this unique shape. The culprit might be another galaxy entirely, like the Small Magellanic Cloud (SMC).

One of our closest neighbors in the Local Group, the SMC, can most often be seen from Australia. That's why it plays a role in many aboriginal folk tales from Australia. The SMC is about 200,000 light years away from the Milky Way (Taylor Tillman, 2018). It has a similarly weird shape, like the LMC, and it's likely the two influenced one another's shapes because they orbit one another. I mean, it does take two to tango. It must be noted, however, that it takes them about 900 million years to finish a single orbit around one another, so... I suppose we can describe that as the slowest tango in the world!

Suppose that you were in possession of the Millennium Falcon from *Star Wars*. First off, that's amazing; go have fun! Second, if the LMC and SMC are among our closest galactic neighbors, how long would it take you to travel to one of them on the Millennium Falcon? Well, the Millennium Falcon can go a little over light speed, so that should cut your journey down to... about 1.5 million years (Howell, 2018). Indeed, that is significantly faster than the two million years that this journey would have taken you on if your speed had been limited to the speed of light, wouldn't it be?

Mysteries in the Milky Way

The idea of going to other galaxies might sound very exciting, but the days when we can do that are very far away. Fortunately, we still have many mysteries to unravel right here in the Milky Way. For example, did you know that stars in the Milky Way generate an odd kind of wave that resembles sound waves? Did you know that these waves make the galaxy literally ring like a bell, assuming you have delicate enough technology to listen to it?

Why is this the case? Honestly, scientists aren't too sure at the moment. One theory is that something, like maybe a dwarf galaxy, collided with the Milky Way at some point in the last 100 million years. Considering the Milky Way's tendency to eat other galaxies, that's entirely possible. So, it's also possible that the stars are still ringing with the impact of that collision. I mean, we're still able to pick up the echoes of the Big Bang, right? Why shouldn't we also be able to hear the ringing of stars post-galactic collision?

The stars' ringing isn't the only mystery in the Milky Way. There are many others, such as the presence of intergalactic clouds. In the Milky Way, there are clouds of hydrogen that move at 32 miles per second, going in all sorts of different directions (Boyle, 2014). They seem to be falling into the galaxy from... we have no idea where! One theory is that these clouds are remnants of the Big Bang. Another is that there may be other objects, like planets, around our galaxy that we haven't spotted yet, and these clouds are somehow coming from them. Still, another theory is that another galaxy that we have yet to identify is puffing them out as it circles around us.

Remember how astronomers were trying to figure out if we had a mysterious Planet 9 in the Milky Way? Well, while they're at it, they're also trying to figure out if there's an invisible Galaxy X that goes with it. Some astronomers think that Planet 9 is actually a part of Galaxy X. They also think that Galaxy X is a dwarf galaxy that we can't see because there's a lot of dust in the way. If only we had an intergalactic duster in our hands! Well, even if we did, we'd probably still have a tough time spotting this Galaxy X because scientists think it's 85% dark matter (Lyons, 2015). So, how will we ever see if the Galaxy X is there? Well, scientists will just have to keep trying new things and inventing new technologies, I suppose. In the meantime, the rest of us could try squinting.

Here's another fascinating mystery for you: Some stars in the Milky Way are moving way faster than normal, and we have no clue why. These stars, which are known as hypervelocity stars, are like superhot, blue giants that jet about 1.6 million miles an hour! Now, that's what I call fast. To be fair, we've only been able to spot one single hypervelocity star in our galaxy, but still. We don't know where it came from or why it's high-tailing the way that it is. Some astronomers think it was somehow created when Sagittarius A, the supermassive black hole at the center of our galaxy, was formed. But who can say?

Out of all the mysteries of the galaxy, which do you think is the most fascinating one? Personally, I'd have to go with black holes. I mean, are they really linked to supposed white holes that can spit you out somewhere else in the universe? If so, where might that somewhere else be? I'd love to find out, though, preferably without having to dive into a black hole myself. There may come a day when someone braves a trip into one, of course, but that day is probably very far away, especially since we don't know where most black holes in the galaxy and universe are. You see, black holes are very, very hard to find because they're kind of impossible to see. Black holes suck anything and everything into them, and that includes light. Without light, we can't really see anything, so...

How do we know black holes even exist, then? If you've asked that question, then you, my friend, will get a gold star! To answer it, we know black holes exist because we can observe how they affect the environment around them. I mean, it's pretty hard to deny a black hole's existence if you can observe a nearby star being sucked into nothingness, right?

Earlier, we'd mentioned that dying stars turn into black holes. Does that mean that the sun will eventually turn into a black hole? Actually, this isn't the case, as only extremely large dying stars undergo transformation into black holes. Don't get me wrong; the sun is pretty big. However, it's not big enough to make the transformation. For example, take supermassive black holes like the one at the center of the Milky Way. Such black holes are usually about 1 million times the size of ordinary suns like ours. Regular black holes aren't quite that big, but they're much larger than our sun, too. Specifically, they're 20 times as big as our sun. So, even if our sun were to suddenly blink out, it would never turn into a black hole.

Did you know that time works really funny in black holes? Say that you were a brave astronaut who decided to dive into one. If you did, time would pass much more slowly for you than it would for the people outside the hole. What feels to them like a minute might be an hour for you, if not much longer?

So, here's a question for you: If black holes exist in the center of galaxies, the way one does in the Milky Way's center, then which came first? Black holes or galaxies? Go ahead and describe how you think the order went and how the first galaxies started to form:

Scientists think that black holes and galaxies sort of came about around the same time. Black holes are born from massive, dying stars. We know that much. That means that stars needed to exist and start dying before the first black holes could form (*Which Came First*, 2024). It stands to reason, then, that the stars came into being first. Around the same time, planets started forming, and things started clustering together here and there. Then, a massive sun somewhere died and turned into a supermassive black hole. This black hole's gravitation pulls started pulling all sorts of star systems, solar systems, planets, and more toward itself, and so the Milky Way formed, as did other galaxies, while the same process repeated itself at their centers over and over again.

Constellation Hunter

Go outside one night and look up at the sky. Up there, you'll see about 6,000 stars, even if you can't quite count them. Did you know that some of these stars form cool patterns called constellations? Did you know you could recognize constellations based on their shapes and use them to navigate? That's what sailors used to do back in the old days before we had Google Maps. They'd look up at the night sky and use constellations to find their way.

Now, the first thing you need to know if you want to be able to recognize constellations, be it to navigate or to just admire them, is that the ones you can see from the northern hemisphere of Earth are different from the ones you can see in the southern hemisphere. That makes sense when you think about it. The northern hemisphere looks at one part of space, after all, and the southern hemisphere looks at another one altogether.

So, what constellations can you learn to spot in the northern and southern hemispheres? First, let's assume you're on the northern half of Earth and look up. The easiest constellation for you to spot from here is the Big Dipper (Chaple, 2008). The Big Dipper is easiest to see on clear spring nights. It's made up of the seven brightest stars. Four of those stars form a kind of bowl; at least, they would if you played Connect the Dots with them. The remaining three stars form the handle of that bowl. So, the Big Dipper kind of looks like a pot with a handle.

Here's a neat trick: Once you've found the Big Dipper, you can actually spot the North Star and the Little Dipper, too. The North Star's scientific name is Polaris. The two stars making up the end of the Big Dipper bowl act as an arrow, pointing the way toward the North Star. That's because they're in line with it (Boeckmann, 2023). Meanwhile, the North Star is at the very tip of the Little Dipper. Specifically, it's the last star making up the handle of the Little Dipper, which is a mirror image of the Big Dipper, only smaller.

Another constellation you can be on the lookout for is Orion, the Hunter. The best time to spot this constellation is on clear winter nights. To find it, you're going to have to search the sky a bit until you come across the three brightest stars, which will all be in line and pretty close together. These three stars will make up Orion's belt. Next, look north of the belt, where you'll find two stars. These will be Orion's shoulders. Lastly, you'll look south for another two stars, which will be Orion's legs.

A good hunter needs a good hunting dog. Luckily, Orion has one. It's called the Great Dog. To find the Great Dog, you'll have to look at Orion's belt and imagine a straight line emerging from it. You'll want to follow this imaginary line to the left until you come across a very bright star. This star will be Sirius. It will also be the Great Dog's snout. In case you're wondering, yes, Sirius the Star is also where Sirius Black from Harry Potter got his name, but I digress. Once you've found Sirius the snout, you'll look beneath it to find three stars forming a triangle. If you did, then voila! You've found your dog's hindquarters.

So, that's it for the northern hemisphere. How about the southern one? There are a number of cool constellations you can find here, too, starting with the Southern Cross. To find the Southern Cross, you are going to have to search the sky for a cross. Surprising, right? The Southern Cross is made up of four stars (Stein, 2022). First, there's Acrux, which makes up the bottom of the cross. Then there's Gacrux, which is at its very top. There is also Mimosa, which has a left-hand tip, and Imai, which has a right-hand tip.

Given the simplicity of its shape, the Southern Cross is pretty easy to spot. I personally find the Jewel Box far more interesting to watch than the Southern Cross, though. The Jewel Box is less of a constellation and more of a star cluster. A cluster of stars, resembling jewels in their sparkle, forms the Jewel Box. These stars are about 6,400 light years away from us and 16 million years old! We can spot it just to the southeast of the star Mimosa, indicating its proximity to the Southern Cross. The Coalsack Nebula is similarly visible.

The Coalsack Nebula is, again, less a constellation and more a very conspicuous dark silhouette in the sky, surrounded by a dusting of stars. It can be found right to the ease of Acrux (Harrington, 2022). What is it, and why is it so dark? Is it some kind of space station or object obscuring our view of the stars? No, actually. The Coal Sack Nebula is a cloud of stardust. It's absolutely massive in size, which is why we can see it without the help of any telescopes or anything like that, despite the fact that it's 600 light years away from Earth! The dust in it is so dense that light cannot go through it, which is why we see it as a black patch.

Spotting all these constellations, clusters, and nebulas is very cool, of course, but here's the thing: They don't exactly answer that one question that has been on humankind's minds since we first looked up at the night sky in wonder. What question might that be, you ask? Why, of course, is it "Are we alone in the universe?" Considering how many billions of stars and galaxies there are in the universe, it seems silly to believe that there is no life anywhere else. Aliens have to exist somewhere in the galaxy or at least in the universe, right? We can't be the only ones. Where, though? Where are these aliens that must exist? Which planets might they be living on, and how might we find them? Of course, let's go right ahead and find out in our next chapter!

Chapter 7:

Worlds Beyond—Discovering

Strange and Wonderful Exoplanets

Did you know that, until 1995, we had no idea there were planets outside our solar system? That seems crazy when you consider how big the galaxy and the universe are. You have to remember, though, that we didn't always have the cool technology we do now. Remember how we said that your smartphone is more powerful than the computer that took humankind to the moon? Well, think about what that means for our ability to observe space beyond our solar system. Only in recent years have we created technology that's advanced enough to be able to do this properly. It's only recently that we've been able to figure out that there are around 4,000 different planets out there, if not many more.

Eight planets make up our solar system, ten if you include Pluto and the alleged Planet 9. We don't refer to planets that exist outside the boundaries of our solar system as planets. They're called "exoplanets." Most exoplanets orbit their own suns, much like Earth does. However, there are exceptions. Indeed, some planets roam freely in space, unencumbered by the gravitational pull of any stars. Obviously, these rogue planets aren't warm enough to have life on them, though. Who knows? Maybe one day they'll be caught by the gravity of a distant star and land just in the perfect position for life to bloom on them. Maybe life did exist on them once upon a time, but it ended after a supernova or something of the sort pushed that planet away from its orbit around a star. That's scary, though, isn't it?

Welcome to the Universe of Exoplanets

Given its massive size, the Milky Way is home to many of the exoplanets that we are aware of. We now have the technology to observe these exoplanets from afar and discover a variety of things about them. For instance, we can measure their size and mass to determine whether they're rocky planets like Earth or gassy planets like Saturn. We can also gain a general understanding of the types of elements present on their surfaces. So, if a planet is very rich in carbon, ice, or iron, we can tell that if we study it enough. Similarly, we can tell if a planet is mostly made of volcanoes, lava, or something of the sort. We've recently come across one exoplanet, for example, that literally has boiling, molten seas, pools, and pools of lava. We've also discovered one that is puffy and only as dense as styrofoam, which kind of means you could break that planet if you were to actually set foot on it! How crazy is that?

So, how exactly do we find exoplanets? How do we spot and identify them? One way we accomplish this is by measuring the dimming of stars. Say that you're looking at a star. The light of that star will dim every time a planet passes in front of it, now, won't it? If this happens regularly, then you can reason that there must be a planet circling it. You can then use your space telescopes to take a closer look and try to find that exoplanet.

Another trick you can use to find exoplanets is called, I kid you not, the wobble method. Have you ever noticed that some stars kind of wobble? If you were to take a look at them using a good telescope, you would. This wobbling, as it turns out, is caused by the gravitational pull of a planet or planets circling that star (*What Is an Exoplanet?* 2021). So, if a star is wobbling, there is probably at least one planet around it! Wait, does that mean our planet causes the sun to wobble? Why, yes, it does, though I'd advise against staring directly at the sun to confirm this, at least if you'd rather your eyes don't water constantly.

Once scientists identify stars with exoplanets around them, they can calculate and figure out things like how hot those planets are based on how close they seem to be to their stars. They can also calculate how much light those planets seem to get. So, what are some of the coolest exoplanets that we've discovered? Well, there are many, to be perfectly honest, but here are some of my favorites:

- **Wasp-76B**

    Wasp-76B may not have the coolest name, but it has a very cool atmosphere. By that, I don't mean that it's cold down there. I mean that this exoplanet literally rains molten iron. So, if anything, things are beyond boiling hot on its surface. Scientists think it gets as hot as 4,532 degrees Fahrenheit on Wasp-76B. They think this is because that's the temperature you need to vaporize, not melt, iron. Without vaporization, iron could turn into rain.

Fortunately, things are a little cooler at night on Wasp-76B. The temperatures drop all the way down to 1,832 degrees Fahrenheit then! This gives the vaporized iron a chance to turn liquid, hence the iron rain.

- **HD 189733-B**

If you think iron rain is cool, then you're in for a real surprise on our next exoplanet, HD 189733-B. HD 189733-B may not have iron rain the way Wasp did, but it does rain glass here! This gassy planet looks beautifully blue from the outside, but that blue isn't from tropical oceans. It's caused by the molten glass rains that regularly happen on the surface. These raindrops don't just pleasantly fall down, either. Instead, they're flung about by the supersonic winds that rage on the exoplanet. As a result, they act more like a shower of bullets than a rain shower. Of course, things are pretty hot on this planet as well. Average temperatures are around 1,700 degrees Fahrenheit. Toasty!

- **Upsilon Andromeda B**

Not every exoplanet is at the mercy of bizarre rain showers. Some are just at the mercy of extreme temperatures. Upsilon Andromeda B is a great example of this. That's why scientists call it the planet of ice and fire. That sounds like the location for the next *Game of Thrones* series, now doesn't it? The thing about Upsilon Andromeda B is that it is lightning-fast, which is why it can orbit its star in just five days! During the day, temperatures average around 2,912 degrees Fahrenheit. At night, however, they drop down to 4 degrees Fahrenheit! Hence, the reference to "ice and fire" from a minute ago!

- **Gliese 1132-B**

Did you know that a planet can have not one but two atmospheres? Well, if you didn't, you're not alone. Scientists weren't aware of this fact either until they discovered Gliese 1132-B. How could a planet have two atmospheres, though? Well, first, there's the planet's regular atmosphere. Then there's the one that is created on the planet thanks to the gravitational influence the exoplanet has on its sun. You see, Gliese 1132-B's gravitational influence on its sun is 20% larger than the influence that the sun's gravity has on the exoplanet. This creates a unique push and pull between the exoplanet and the sun. This push and pull actually squeezes and stretches the exoplanet! As a result of this flex, a lot of volcanic activity happens on the planet, and lots of gases are released into the atmosphere. So, these gases gather together on a separate level, creating a whole second atmosphere for the planet!

The Search for Habitable Worlds

Obviously, none of these extremely cool planets are exactly habitable. If they somehow happen to have life on them, that would be extremely impressive. I mean, it would be pretty hard to find a lifeform that can withstand iron rains and supersonic winds, right? Does that mean we haven't found any habitable planets, though? Not really. In fact, NASA has managed to identify several exoplanets that may be capable of supporting life. Now, it should be emphasized here that "habitable" doesn't mean "yes, there are aliens on them." Rather, it means these exoplanets MAY have the right conditions to support life.

Kepler-20e is the first known habitable exoplanet. We discovered Kepler-20e in December 2011, and it appears to be a rocky planet similar to Earth. It's a bit smaller than Earth, but it's closer to its sun than Mercury is to ours. It's a fast exoplanet, too, as it only takes 6.1 days to complete a single orbit around the sun. The distance between it and its sun from our solar system is approximately 921.4 light-years, which is quite close.

The one problem with Kepler-20e? It's kind of scorching hot, so much so that it's hard to find water in liquid form on the planet. Fortunately, scientists have only identified Kepler-20e as the first potentially habitable planet. There are others, like Kepler 22-b (Brennan, n.d.). Yes, all potentially habitable planets bear the name Kepler. The reason for this is that we usually name planets after the device that discovered them. In the Keplers' case, this device is the Kepler Space Telescope.

With that out of the way, let's get back to Kepler 22-b. Kepler 22-b is a kind of super-Earth in that it seems to be very similar to Earth but is much, much bigger than it. You can fit about two Earths into Kepler 22-b (Brennan, n.d.). Because of its size, scientists aren't sure if it's actually a rocky planet or a gassy one. From a distance, it looks like some kind of massive ocean, and its average temperatures are around 60 degrees Fahrenheit. That's very livable!

There are two other Kepler exoplanets that might turn out to be habitable. The first of these is Kepler 186-f (Brennan, 2009). Kepler 186-f is just about the same size as Earth, and it orbits a red dwarf sun. It takes Kepler 186-f 121 days to finish its orbit around that sun, and it's one of five planets within that specific solar system, which is about 181 light years away from us. Likely a rocky planet, it was discovered in 2014.

The last potentially habitable planet is Kepler 452-b. This poetically named exoplanet is about 60% larger than Earth. While Kepler 452-b does look livable, we don't yet know whether it has continents and oceans the way our home, the Earth, does (*NASA's Kepler Mission Discovers Bigger, Older Cousin to Earth*, 2015). What we do know is that it takes 382 days to orbit its sun, which is much closer to our 365 days down here on the ground. Kepler 452-b's star is smaller and cooler, though, so if we want to see whether there's life on it, we are going to have to take a much, much closer look. Road trip, anyone?

Before we all board our spaceships, I have one question for you: What makes a planet habitable? What are the criteria for habitability? To be habitable means to be able to host life for a long period of time. Based on all you know and have learned, how would you define a habitable planet:

Based on that definition, how about you design a habitable planet somewhere in the distance? You can both write about this imaginary planet and draw it if you'd like. You can even name it something other than "Kepler." So, what are you going to be naming your very own planet? What is it going to look like? More importantly, when can we move there?

Conclusion

Having explored the farthest reaches of the universe, I think it's finally time to head back home to Earth with lots of cool stories to tell, having made one tremendous discovery after another. Your friends and family are eagerly waiting for you to return, I'm sure, and tell them all about the wonders of the universe you've uncovered. You've uncovered so many, too, so where will you begin? Are you going to take things in chronological order and start talking about the Big Bang? Instead, are you going to start with our sun and how it formed from all that helium and hydrogen? Perhaps you'll keep things more grounded at first and begin by discussing how Earth formed and developed all sorts of interesting ecosystems, giving rise to unique forms of life.

Maybe that doesn't float your boat, though. Maybe you're far more interested in exploring our solar system, seeing as it is filled with some mesmerizing planets and moons. If so, you might start with the dwarf planet Pluto, which got demoted from its official status some years ago. Alternatively, you might start talking about Mars since we human beings intend to head there in the next 20 years or so. Can you imagine how exciting the day will be when we finally get to do that?

What if you don't want to stop with just our solar system? What if you prefer to focus on the horizon and consider a broader perspective? If so, you can start off by weaving tales of the Milky Way. The Milky Way galaxy is kind of massive, after all. It isn't the most massive thing in the universe, though. So, if your motto is "Go big or go home," then talking about our neighbor galaxies and the mysteries that populate the universe, like primordial black holes, white holes, and rogue planets, might be the way to go.

Are you more interested in planets outside of the solar system? Well, I can't blame you, seeing as some of them have things like iron rain, glass rain, and two atmospheres. Perhaps such things really might be a better starting point for your tale of discovery. I have to say, though, that if you're going to be telling your friends about exoplanets, then diving into the potentially habitable ones, ones that might have alien life on them, seems just as exciting to me. At the very least, that can turn into a debate about what aliens look like, can't it? After all, whoever said aliens have to be little and green?

So, what do you think? Where do you want to begin talking about your incredible adventures? More importantly, how do you want to continue them? The universe is filled with so many wonders and secrets that what we've learned here today is just the beginning. There are so many more things to see and wonder about. So, why not keep exploring? Who knows what kind of other marvels you'll unearth or, rather, un-universe along the way?

Glossary

Atmosphere: A shield of gases that are wrapped around a planet, such as Earth.

Black hole: A place in space that forms after a massive star collapses and that has a gravitational pull so strong that it pulls anything that's nearby inside itself, including light.

Ecosystem: A biological community of different kinds of organisms and living beings that co-exist in balance in a given environment.

Exoplanet: Any planet that orbits a sun other than the one in our solar system.

Galaxy: A system that's made up of millions to billions of stars, as well as stardust and gas clouds.

Gravity: The force that planets, moons, and other similar space objects have that attracts and pulls objects toward themselves.

Microgravity: Gravity that's so low you can float in it.

Orbit: The round or elliptical path that a planet winds around the sun or that a moon winds around a planet.

Planet: A space object that maintains an elliptical or round orbit around the sun in a solar system.

Primordial black hole: Black holes that have formed in the immediate aftermath of the Big Bang.

Solar system: The gathering of planets and moons that orbit a sun thanks to its gravitational pull.

Universe: Literally everything that will ever exist out in space.

References

Boeckmann, C. (2023, December 4). *Stargazing: Finding the stars and constellations*. Old Farmer's Almanac. https://www.almanac.com/content/stargazing-finding-stars-and-constellations

Boyle, A. (2014, July 1). *10 galactic mysteries of the Milky Way*. Listverse. https://listverse.com/2014/07/01/10-galactic-mysteries-of-the-milky-way/

Brennan, P. (n.d.). *Kepler-22b*. NASA Exoplanet Exploration: Planets beyond Our Solar System. https://exoplanets.nasa.gov/exoplanet-catalog/1599/kepler-22b/

Brennan, P. (2009). *Kepler-186f, the first Earth-size planet in the habitable zone (artist's concept) - exoplanet exploration: Planets beyond our solar system*. NASA Exoplanet Exploration: Planets beyond Our Solar System. https://exoplanets.nasa.gov/resources/198/kepler-186f-the-first-earth-size-planet-in-the-habitable-zone-artists-concept/

Brown, T. (2024, March 20). *Photosynthesis*. National Geographic Society. https://education.nationalgeographic.org/resource/photosynthesis

Butler, T. (2020, April 8). *Create your own mini ecosystem at home!* Shaver's Creek Environmental Center. https://www.shaverscreek.org/2020/04/08/create-your-own-mini-ecosystem-at-home/

Chaple, G. (2008, March 10). *Learn the constellations*. Astronomy Magazine. https://www.astronomy.com/observing/learn-the-constellations/

Choi, C. Q. (2017a, September 8). *Moon facts: Fun information about the earth's moon*. Space. https://www.space.com/55-earths-moon-formation-composition-and-orbit.html

Choi, C. Q. (2017b, October 18). *Planet uranus: Facts about its name, moons and orbit*. Space. https://www.space.com/45-uranus-seventh-planet-in-earths-solar-system-was-first-discovered-planet.html

Choi, C. Q. (2019, May 13). *Saturn: Facts about the ringed planet*. Space. https://www.space.com/48-saturn-the-solar-systems-major-ring-bearer.html

Choi, C. Q., & Dobrijevic, D. (2017, October 14). *Planet Mercury: Facts about the planet closest to the sun*. Space. https://www.space.com/36-mercury-the-suns-closest-planetary-neighbor.html

Chown, M. (2024, February 28). *7 questions about the expansion of the Universe*. Sky at Night Magazine. https://www.skyatnightmagazine.com/space-science/expansion-universe

Couture, E. (2015, September 18). *10 Facts about the Milky Way*. Planetarium and Astronomy Center - University of Maine. https://astro.umaine.edu/10-facts-about-the-milky-way/

Dalcanton, J. (2012). *The Milky Way Galaxy*. American Museum of Natural History. https://www.amnh.org/explore/ology/astronomy/the-milky-way-galaxy2

Dutfield, S., & Gammon, K. (2019, February 8). *Terrestrial planets: Definition & facts about the inner planets.* Space. https://www.space.com/17028-terrestrial-planets.html

Freeman, L. (n.d.). *What would happen if you fell into a black hole?* BBC Earth. https://www.bbcearth.com/news/what-would-happen-if-you-fell-into-a-black-hole

Gaughan, R. (2018). *The moon's effect on the seasons.* Sciencing. https://sciencing.com/moons-effect-seasons-22257.html

Graham cracker plate tectonics. (2015, September 9). Playdough to Plato. https://www.playdoughtoplato.com/graham-cracker-plate-tectonics/

Greshko, M. (2018, September 10). *Planet Earth, explained.* National Geographic. https://www.nationalgeographic.com/science/article/earth

Hamer, A. (2019, August 1). *What would happen if the sun disappeared?* Discovery. https://www.discovery.com/science/What-Would-Happen If the Sun-Disappeared

Harrington, P. (2022, September 9). *101 must-see cosmic objects: The Coalsack Nebula.* Astronomy Magazine. https://www.astronomy.com/observing/101-must-see-cosmic-objects-the-coalsack-nebula/

Howell, E. (2018, July 2). *It would take 200,000 years at light speed to cross the milky way.* Space. https://www.space.com/41047-milky-way-galaxy-size-bigger-than-thought.html

Howell, E., & May, A. (2023, July 26). *What is the big bang theory?* Space. https://www.space.com/25126-big-bang-theory.html

Jupiter. (n.d.). NASA Science. https://science.nasa.gov/jupiter/

Klesman, A. (2018, December 12). *How did the first element form after the big bang?* Astronomy Magazine. https://www.astronomy.com/science/how-did-the-first-element-form-after-the-big-bang/

Krofcheck, D. (2009, October 22). *How elements are formed.* Science Learning Hub. https://www.sciencelearn.org.nz/resources/1727-how-elements-are-formed

Lyons, A. (2015, February 27). *10 fun facts about black holes.* Planetarium and Astronomy Center - University of Maine. https://astro.umaine.edu/10-fun-facts-about-black-holes/

NASA's Kepler mission discovers bigger, older cousin to Earth. (2015, July 23). The National Aeronautics and Space Administration. https://www.nasa.gov/news-release/nasas-kepler-mission-discovers-bigger-older-cousin-to-earth/

Neptune: Facts. (2023). NASA Science. https://science.nasa.gov/neptune/facts/

Nikola Sakay, Y. (2021, April 7). *Ingenuity and beyond: 10 milestones in space exploration.* Daily Sabah. https://www.dailysabah.com/life/science/ingenuity-and-beyond-10-milestones-in-space-exploration

Planet Mars. (2019). NASA's Mars Exploration Program. https://mars.nasa.gov/all-about-mars/facts/

Pluto: Facts. (2023). NASA Science. https://science.nasa.gov/dwarf-planets/pluto/facts/

Powys Whyte, K. (2024, February 2). *Why do different places on earth have different climates.* Tribal Climate Map. https://www.tribalclimatecamp.org/why-do-different-places-on-earth-have-different-climates/

Racine County Eye Staff. (2024, March 28). *Space tourism: Bridging science fiction with scientific reality | racine county eye*. Racine County Eye. https://racinecountyeye.com/2024/03/28/space-tourism-bridging-science-fiction-with-scientific-reality/

Rafi Letzter. (2019, October). *Is our solar system's mysterious "planet 9" really a grapefruit-size black hole?* Live Science. https://www.livescience.com/tiny-ancient-black-hole-planet-nine.html

Rutledge, K., McDaniel, M., Teng , S., Hall , H., Ramroop , T., Sprout, E., Hunt, J., Boudreau, D., & Costa, H. (2023, May 1). *Ecosystem*. National Geographic Society. https://education.nationalgeographic.org/resource/ecosystem/

Rutledge, K., McDaniel, M., Teng , S., Hall, H., Ramroop , T., Sprout, E., Hunt, J., Boudreau , D., & Costa, H. (2023). *Landform*. National Geographic Society. https://education.nationalgeographic.org/resource/landform/

Schilling, G. (2023, April 29). *How astronomers can observe the afterglow of the Big Bang*. Sky at Night Magazine. https://www.skyatnightmagazine.com/space-science/afterglow-of-big-bang

Stein, V. (2022, November 3). *Exploring the famous southern cross constellation*. Space. https://www.space.com/29445-southern-cross-constellation-skywatching.html

Sukheja, B. (2022, September 22). *"The sun is actually white": Ex NASA astronaut confirms space fact*. NDTV. https://www.ndtv.com/world-news/the-sun-is-actually-white-ex-nasa-astronaut-confirms-space-fact-3340514

Tambe, N. (2023, May 31). *How to become an astronaut? (2023 guide)*. Forbes Advisor INDIA.

https://www.forbes.com/advisor/in/education/how-to-become-an-astronaut/

Tammy. (n.d.). *How to make a barometer.* Housing a Forest. http://www.housingaforest.com/how-to-make-a-barometer/

Taylor Tillman, N. (2018, December 13). *Small Magellanic Cloud: A satellite dwarf galaxy neighbor.* Space. https://www.space.com/42732-small-magellanic-cloud.html

Turgeon, A., & Morse, E. (2023, March 6). *Sun.* National Geographic Society. https://education.nationalgeographic.org/resource/sun/

Venus: Facts. (2024). NASA Science. https://science.nasa.gov/venus/facts/

Warren, S. (n.d.). *How the Earth and moon formed, explained.* University of Chicago News. https://news.uchicago.edu/explainer/formation-earth-and-moon-explained

What is an exoplanet? (2021, April 2). Exoplanet Exploration: Planets beyond Our Solar System. https://exoplanets.nasa.gov/what-is-an-exoplanet/overview/

What is the big bang? (2021, March 17). NASA Space Place – NASA Science for Kids. https://spaceplace.nasa.gov/big-bang/en/

What is the greenhouse effect? (n.d.). American Museum of Natural History. https://www.amnh.org/explore/ology/climate-change/what-is-the-greenhouse-effect

Which came first: Black holes or galaxies? (2024, February 6). ScienceDaily. https://www.sciencedaily.com/releases/2024/02/240206144917.htm

Why does the atmosphere not drift off into space? (n.d.). NOAA SciJinks – All about Weather. https://scijinks.gov/pressure/

Young, C. (2021, October 21). *The Milky Way is eating a galaxy that's already swallowed another one.* Interesting Engineering. https://interestingengineering.com/science/the-milky-way-is-eating-a-galaxy-thats-already-swallowed-another-one

Image References

51581. (2014, December 9). *Solar System Planets.* [Image]. Pixabay. https://pixabay.com/photos/solar-system-sun-mercury-venus-439046/

D. Van Rensburg. *Exoplanet Planet.* [Image]. Pixabay. https://pixabay.com/photos/exoplanet-planet-space-astronomy-7414128/

Geralt. (2015, August 13). *Space Science Fiction.* [Image]. Pixabay. https://pixabay.com/illustrations/space-science-fiction-cosmos-911785/

Geralt. (2018, April 16). *Universe Stars.* [Image]. Pixabay. https://pixabay.com/photos/universe-heaven-stars-space-cosmos-3324227/

Liming0759. (2019, December 3). *Landform Earth.* [Image]. Pixabay. https://pixabay.com/photos/landform-earth-forest-scenery-color-4667814/

Melmak. (2015, April 24). Habitable Exoplanet. [Image]. Pixabay. https://pixabay.com/photos/space-exoplanet-interstellar-736712/

NASA Imagery. (2010, December 5). *Space Station Moon Walk*. [Image]. Pixabay. https://pixabay.com/photos/space-walk-astronaut-nasa-aerospace-991/

Terranaut. (2023, January 7). *Exoplanet*. [Image]. Pixabay. https://pixabay.com/photos/cosmos-universe-moon-planet-7700335/

The Heart of Sound. (2017, February 10). *Starry Sky Milky Way*. [Image]. Pixabay. https://pixabay.com/photos/starry-sky-milky-way-night-sky-2051448/

V. Jacob. (2013, October 30). *Sea Ecosystem*. [Image]. Pixabay. https://pixabay.com/photos/christmastree-worms-close-up-coral-202320/

Wiki Images. (2011a, December 14). *Astronaut Space Suit*. [Image]. Pixabay. https://pixabay.com/photos/astronaut-space-suit-space-universe-11080/

Wiki Images. (2011b, December 15). *Big Bang Galaxy*. [Image]. Pixabay. https://pixabay.com/photos/galaxy-big-bang-explosion-space-11188/

Wiki Images. (2011c, December 15). *Earth*. [Image]. Pixabay. https://pixabay.com/photos/earth-globe-planet-world-space-11015/

Wiki Images. (2011d, December 15). *Orion Nebula*. [Image]. Pixabay. https://pixabay.com/photos/orion-nebula-emission-nebula-11107/

Wiki Images. (2012a, January 9). *Mercury Planet*. [Image]. Pixabay. https://pixabay.com/photos/mercury-planet-surface-solar-system-11591/

Wiki Images. (2012b, October 30). *Moon Landing*. [Image]. Pixabay. https://pixabay.com/photos/space-station-moon-landing-apollo-15-60615/

Wiki Images. (2012c, January 9). *Sun in Space*. [Image]. Pixabay. https://pixabay.com/photos/sun-solar-flare-space-outer-space-11582/

Wiki Images. (2013a, January 24). *Milky Way*. [Image]. Pixabay. https://pixabay.com/photos/milky-way-nebula-galaxy-stars-74005/

Wiki Images. (2013b, January 3). *Neptune Planet*. [Image]. Pixabay. https://pixabay.com/photos/neptune-planet-solar-system-67537/

Wiki Images. (2013c, January 4). *Rocket Launch*. [Image]. Pixabay. https://pixabay.com/photos/rocket-launch-rocket-take-off-67643/

Made in United States
Troutdale, OR
11/21/2024

25142574R00062